THE SINGULARITY PRINCIPLES

Anticipating
and managing
cataclysmically
disruptive technologies

by
David W. Wood
Chair, London Futurists

Copyright © 2022 David W. Wood

All rights reserved

The moral rights of the author have been asserted

Paperback ISBN 978-0-9954942-6-8

Published by Delta Wisdom

The Singularity Principles on one page

Anticipating and managing cataclysmically disruptive technologies
NBIC: Nanotech Biotech, Infotech, Cognotech
→ AGI → Superintelligence → The Singularity

Analysing goals and potential outcomes:	Desirable characteristics of tech solutions:
Question desirability	*Reject opacity*
Clarify externalities	*Promote resilience*
Require peer reviews	*Promote verifiability*
Involve multiple perspectives	*Promote auditability*
Analyse whole system	*Clarify risks to users*
Anticipate fat tails	*Clarify trade-offs*
Ensuring development takes place responsibly:	**Evolution & enforcement:**
Insist on accountability	*Build consensus regarding principles*
Penalise disinformation	*Provide incentives to address omissions*
Design for cooperation	*Halt development if principles not upheld*
Analyse via simulations	*Consolidate progress via legal frameworks*
Maintain human oversight	

Context: Ten essential observations

Tech breakthroughs are unpredictable (both timing and impact)
Potential complex interactions make prediction even harder
Changes in human attributes complicate tech changes
Greater tech power enables more devastating results (good/bad)
Different perspectives assess "good" vs. "bad" differently
Competition can be hazardous as well as beneficial
Some tech failures would be too drastic to allow recovery
A history of good results is no guarantee of future success
It's insufficient to rely on good intentions
Wishful thinking predisposes blindness to problems

"An excellent and detailed introduction to the AI Safety problem, the Singularity, and our options for the future."

Roman Yampolskiy, Professor of Computer Science, The University of Louisville

"It truly is gratifying to see deep thought on these crucial issues."

David Brin, Science fiction author and scientist, Winner of Nebula, Locus, Campbell, and Hugo Awards

"One of the most important books that you will read this decade, which David Wood calls 'The Decade of Confusion'. The 2020s bring us to the cusp of a transformation in human civilization quite unlike any we have previously experienced. David's book is an essential handbook to aid you in navigating this transformation."

Ted Shelton, Expert Partner, Automation and Digital Innovation, Bain and Company

"*The Singularity Principles* is an absorbing, comprehensive overview of the challenges I truly believe we will soon face as AGI arrives. Are we intellectually and emotionally ready to have serious discussions about it?"

Patty O'Callaghan, Google's Women Techmakers Ambassador

"No Solarpunk or regenerative movement activist should ignore this brilliant futurist's book on the Singularity. It is neither techno-fetishist nor in denial of its coming!"

George Pór, Founder and Director of Research, Future HOW

"I have followed David's work for nearly twenty years. It's great to see him taking his thinking to the next level. AGI is arriving faster than many expected. It's vital to raise the calibre of the discussion on AGI and on the Singularity. That's what this timely, valuable book achieves."

Ajit Jaokar, Visiting Fellow and Course Director, Artificial Intelligence: Cloud and Edge Implementations, University of Oxford

"David Wood is a man of great intellect which shines through in this erudite analysis of the potential benefits and costs of cataclysmically disruptive technologies. David's Singularity Principles provide a strong basis for the critical tasks of the anticipation and management of alternative outcomes. I commend this book most warmly to friends and colleagues alike."

Hugh Shields, Chairman and Founder, The Centre for Research into AI and Mankind

"Various world disruptions are escalating in a way that begs the thought 'if only we had started serious work on this decades ago'. The pain in years to come will be more severe or catastrophic if we continue as we have. Conversely, if we actively manage things the reward is significantly greater human flourishing. The Singularity Principles form a good framework of behaviours to produce better outcomes than we get from development as currently run. They should be brought to the attention of anyone wishing to improve the way they do things."

Peter Jackson, Software Consultant, change management and configuration management

"David's book provides a powerful overview of what's ahead of us, and thoughtfully describes the opportunities and challenges brought on by the rise of exponential technologies. A must-read for anyone that is looking to increase their Future-Readiness."

Gerd Leonhard, Futurist, CEO The Futures Agency, Author and Film Maker, *The Good Future*

"Black box AIs are being spawned every week and as much money and computer power that is available is being poured into them as fast as possible. We are deep into the rapids and heading for the vertical chute. Is there still time to educate the public? This book needs to be read by a wide audience immediately – especially by those few people who have actual control over the final few steering manoeuvres remaining for AI development."

Jonathan Cole, Radiative Cooling Engineer, technologically advanced canopies and systems

"I have just finished reading the manuscript of *The Singularity is Nearer* to be published in 2023 by my friend Ray Kurzweil. Kurzweil's new book is very optimistic and ratifies his forecast to reach the technological singularity by 2045. In order to have a positive singularity and flourishing human future, I also highly recommend reading *The Singularity Principles* so that we avoid most of the hellish scenario and achieve most of the heavenly scenario. David Wood has scored another fantastic book, full of brilliant ideas and great examples."

José Luis Cordeiro, Founding Faculty, Singularity University

"This really is an urgent call to action #AIforGood."

> **David Levin**, University Entrepreneur in Residence, Arizona State University, and Supervisory Board Chairman, The Learning Network

"David Wood regularly features as a panellist at World Talent Economic Forum events. I always enjoy his contributions, particularly his insights about the future of AI, which you can read about in *The Singularity Principles*."

> **Sharif Uddin Ahmed Rana**, Founder and President, World Talent Economy Forum

"We are witnessing disruptive technologies with an ever-increasing rate of emergence and societal impact. The rise of Artificial General Intelligence presents the possibility of both the most profound benefits and dangers to humanity. There are no historical precedents; no magic formulae to guarantee success. However, *The Singularity Principles* can guide us as we manage these potent technologies and produce a desired beneficial future."

> **David Shumaker**, Director of Applied Innovation, US Transhumanist Party & Transhuman Club

"This important book shines light on looming, potentially irreversible, threats of AI, counterbalanced with pragmatic guidance towards a vision rich with AI opportunities. David Wood provides a prescient call to action, raising awareness and cutting through the confusion."

> **Alan Boulton**, Senior Software Engineer Socionext Europe GmbH

"I cannot stress strongly enough how important this book is – for our own mental health, but also for the health of our species. Real challenges are fast approaching. How we deal with them collectively will mean the difference between a very bright future or a potential cataclysm. Whilst the latter does not sound very hopeful, the path to the former is well discussed, which gives me real hope that humankind could have a very bright future indeed!"

Iain Beveridge, Director, Telepresent

*The cover of this book incorporates a design "space-5751707" by Pixabay member **Ebenezer42** (Phillip Schmidtke), used with many thanks!*

Table of Contents

Preface	**1**
Confusion, turbulence, and peril	2
This time it's different	3
The scope of the Principles	5
Collective insight	7
The short form of the Principles	8
The four areas covered by the Principles	9
1. Ten essential observations	**11**
Tech breakthroughs are unpredictable (both timing and impact)	11
Potential complex interactions make prediction even harder	12
Changes in human attributes complicate tech changes	12
Greater tech power enables more devastating results	13
Different perspectives assess "good" vs. "bad" differently	14
Competition can be hazardous as well as beneficial	14
Some tech failures would be too drastic to allow recovery	15
A history of good results is no guarantee of future success	15
It's insufficient to rely on good intentions	16
Wishful thinking predisposes blindness to problems	16
2. Fast-changing technologies: risks and benefits	**17**
Technology risk factors	18
Prioritising benefits?	20
What about ethics?	22
The transhumanist stance	24
2.1 Special complications with AI	**27**
Problems with training data	27

The black box nature of AI	29
Interactions between multiple algorithms	30
Self-improving AI	33
Devious AI	35
Four catastrophic error modes	36
The broader perspective	38
2.2 The AI Control Problem	**41**
The gorilla problem	41
Examples of dangers with uncontrollable AI	43
Proposed solutions (which don't work)	47
The impossibility of full verification	48
Emotion misses the point	49
No off switch	51
The ineffectiveness of tripwires	52
Escaping from confinement	53
The ineffectiveness of restrictions	55
No automatic super ethics	57
Issues with hard-wiring ethical guidelines	59
2.3 The AI Alignment Problem	**63**
Asimov's Three Laws	64
Ethical dilemmas and trade-offs	65
Problems with proxies	68
The gaming of proxies	70
Simple examples of profound problems	71
Humans disagree	73
No automatic super ethics (again)	74
Other options for answers?	75
2.4 No easy solutions	**77**

No guarantees from the free market	77
No guarantees from cosmic destiny	79
Planet B?	81
Humans merging with AI?	82
Approaching the Singularity	83

3. What is the Singularity? — 85

Breaking down the definition	85
Four alternative definitions	89
Four possible routes to the Singularity	93
The Singularity and AI self-awareness	96
Singularity timescales	97
Positive and negative singularities	100
Tripwires and canary signals	102
Moving forward	103

3.1 The Singularitarian Stance — 105

AGI is possible	108
AGI could happen within just a few decades	111
Winner takes all	115
The difficulty of controlling AGI	116
Superintelligence and superethics	118
Not the Terminator	119
Recap	121
Opposition to the Singularitarian Stance	122

3.2 A complication: the Singularity Shadow — 123

Singularity timescale determinism	124
Singularity outcome determinism	126
Singularity hyping	127
Singularity risk complacency	129

Singularity term overloading	130
Singularity anti-regulation fundamentalism	131
Singularity preoccupation	133
Looking forward	136

3.3 The denial of the Singularity — 137

The denial of death	138
How special is the human mind?	139
A credible positive vision	141

4. The question of urgency — 143

Factors causing AI to improve	144
15 options on the table	146
The difficulty of measuring progress	153
Learning from Christopher Columbus	157
The possibility of fast take-off	161

5. The Principles in depth — 165

5.1 Analysing goals and potential outcomes — 167

Question desirability	168
Clarify externalities	170
Require peer reviews	171
Involve multiple perspectives	172
Analyse the whole system	173
Anticipate fat tails	174

5.2 Desirable characteristics of tech solutions — 177

Reject opacity	177
Promote resilience	179
Promote verifiability	179
Promote auditability	181

Clarify risks to users	182
Clarify trade-offs	183
5.3 Ensuring development takes place responsibly	**185**
Insist on accountability	185
Penalise disinformation	186
Design for cooperation	187
Analyse via simulations	187
Maintain human oversight	189
5.4 Evolution and enforcement	**191**
Build consensus regarding principles	191
Provide incentives to address omissions	192
Halt development if principles are not upheld	193
Consolidate progress via legal frameworks	195
6. Key success factors	**197**
Public understanding	197
Persistent urgency	198
Reliable action against noncompliance	199
Public funding	200
International support	201
A sense of inclusion and collaboration	202
7. Questions arising	**203**
7.1 Measuring human flourishing	**205**
Some example trade-offs	206
Updating the Universal Declaration of Human Rights	208
Constructing an Index of Human and Social Flourishing	209
7.2 Trustable monitoring	**211**
Moore's Law of Mad Scientists	211

Four projects to reduce the dangers of WMDs	213
Detecting mavericks	213
Examples of trustable monitoring	215
Watching the watchers	216

7.3 Uplifting politics — 219

Uplifting regulators	220
The central role of politics	221
Toward superdemocracy	224
Technology improving politics	225
Transcending party politics	227
The prospects for political progress	229

7.4 Uplifting education — 231

Top level areas of the Vital Syllabus	233
Improving the Vital Syllabus	234

7.5 To AGI or not AGI? — 235

Global action against the creation of AGI?	235
Possible alternatives to AGI?	236
A dividing line between AI and AGI?	238
A practical proposal	240

7.6 Measuring progress toward AGI — 241

Aggregating expert opinions	243
Metaculus predictions	245
Alternative canary signals for AGI	249
AI index reports	250

7.7 Growing a coalition of the willing — 251

Risks and actions	253

Endnotes — 255

Preface

This book is dedicated to what may be the most important concept in human history, namely, the Singularity – what it is, what it is *not*, the steps by which we may reach it, and, crucially, how to make it more likely that we'll experience a *positive singularity* rather than a *negative singularity*.

For now, here's a simple definition. The Singularity is the emergence of Artificial General Intelligence (AGI), and the associated transformation of the human condition. Spoiler alert: that transformation will be profound. But if we're not paying attention, it's likely to be *profoundly bad*.

Despite the importance of the concept of the Singularity, the subject receives nothing like the attention it deserves. When it *is* discussed, it often receives scorn or ridicule. Alas, you'll hear sniggers and see eyes rolling.

That's because, as I'll explain, there's a kind of shadow around the concept – an unhelpful set of distortions that make it harder for people to fully perceive the real opportunities and the real risks that the Singularity brings.

These distortions grow out of a wider confusion – confusion about the complex interplay of forces that are leading society to the adoption of ever-more powerful technologies, including ever-more powerful AI.

It's my task in this book to dispel the confusion, to untangle the distortions, to highlight practical steps forward, and to attract much more serious attention to the Singularity. The future of humanity is at stake.

Let's start with the confusion.

Confusion, turbulence, and peril

The 2020s could be called *the Decade of Confusion*. Never before has so much information washed over everyone, leaving us, all too often, overwhelmed, intimidated, and distracted. Former certainties have dimmed. Long-established alliances have fragmented. Flurries of excitement have pivoted quickly to chaos and disappointment. These are turbulent times.

However, if we could see through the confusion, distraction, and intimidation, what we should notice is that human flourishing is, potentially, poised to soar to unprecedented levels. Fast-changing technologies are on the point of providing a string of remarkable benefits. We are near the threshold of radical improvements to health, nutrition, security, creativity, collaboration, intelligence, awareness, and enlightenment – *with these improvements being available to everyone.*

Unfortunately, these same fast-changing technologies also threaten multiple sorts of disaster. These technologies are two-edged swords. Unless we wield them with great skill, they are likely to spin out of control. If we remain overwhelmed, intimidated, and distracted, our prospects are poor. Accordingly, these are *perilous* times.

These dual future possibilities – technology-enabled sustainable superabundance, versus technology-induced catastrophe – have featured in numerous discussions that I have chaired at London Futurists meetups[1] going all the way back to March 2008[2].

As these discussions have progressed, year by year, I have gradually formulated and refined what I now call the Singularity Principles. These principles are intended:

- To steer humanity's relationships with fast-changing technologies,
- To manage multiple risks of disaster,
- To enable the attainment of remarkable benefits,
- And, thereby, to help humanity approach a profoundly positive singularity.

In short, the Singularity Principles are intended to counter today's widespread confusion, distraction, and intimidation, by providing clarity, credible grounds for hope, and an urgent call to action.

This time it's different

I first introduced the Singularity Principles, under that name and with the same general format, in the final chapter, "Singularity", of my 2021 book *Vital Foresight: The Case for Active Transhumanism*[3]. That chapter is the culmination of a 642-page book. The preceding sixteen chapters of that book set out at some length the challenges and opportunities that these principles need to address.

Since the publication of *Vital Foresight*, it has become evident to me that the Singularity Principles require a short, focused book of their own. That's what you now hold in your hands.

The Singularity Principles is by no means the only new book on the subject of the management of powerful disruptive technologies. The public, thankfully, are waking up to the need to understand these technologies better, and numerous authors are responding to that need. As one example, the phrase "Artificial Intelligence", forms part of the title of scores of new books.

I have personally learned many things from some of these recent books. However, to speak frankly, I find myself dissatisfied by the prescriptions these authors have advanced. These authors generally fail to appreciate the full extent of the threats and opportunities ahead. And even if they do see the true scale of these issues, the recommendations these authors propose strike me as being inadequate.

Therefore, I cannot keep silent.

Accordingly, I present in this new book the content of the Singularity Principles, brought up to date in the light of recent debates and new insights. The book also covers:

- Why the Singularity Principles are sorely needed
- The source and design of these principles
- The significance of the term "Singularity"
- Why there is so much unhelpful confusion about "the Singularity"
- What's different about the Singularity Principles, compared to recommendations of other analysts
- The kinds of outcomes expected if these principles are followed
- The kinds of outcomes expected if these principles are *not* followed
- How you – dear reader – can, and should, become involved, finding your place in a growing coalition
- How these principles are likely to evolve further
- How these principles can be put into practice, all around the world – *with the help of people like you.*

The scope of the Principles

To start with, the Singularity Principles can and should be applied to the anticipation and management of the NBIC technologies that are at the heart of the current, fourth, industrial revolution. NBIC – nanotech, biotech, infotech, and cognotech – is a quartet of four interlinked technological disruptions which are likely to grow significantly stronger as the 2020s unfold:

- **Nanotech** can provide resilient new materials, new processes for manufacturing and recycling, new ways to capture and distribute energy, new types of computing hardware, and pervasive new low-cost surveillance networks of all-seeing sensors
- **Infotech** can draw unexpected inferences from large datasets, leaping over human capabilities in increasing numbers of domains of thought, and displacing greater numbers of human employees from tasks which used to occupy large parts of their paid employment
- **Biotech** enables the modification not only of nature, but of *human* nature: it will allow us not only to create new types of lifeforms – synthetic organisms that can outperform those found in nature – but also to edit the human metabolism much more radically than is possible via existing tools such as vaccinations, antibiotics, and occasional organ transplants
- **Cognotech** allows similar modifications for the human mind, brain, and spirit, conceivably enabling in just a few short weeks the kind of

changes in mindset and inner character which previously might have required many years of disciplined practice of yoga, meditation, and/or therapy; it also enables alarming new types of mind control and ego manipulation.

Each of these four technological disruptions has the potential to fundamentally transform large parts of the human experience.

Looking beyond NBIC, the Singularity Principles can and should *also* be applied to the anticipation and management of the core technology that will likely give rise to a *fifth* industrial revolution, namely the technology of AGI (artificial general intelligence), and the rapid additional improvements in artificial superintelligence that will likely follow fast on the footsteps of AGI.

Artificial superintelligence will exceed human capabilities, not just in individual fields of mental reasoning, but in *all* fields of mental reasoning.

The emergence of AGI is known as the technological singularity – or, more briefly, as *the* Singularity.

In other words, the Singularity Principles apply both:

- To the longer-term lead-up to the Singularity, from today's fast-improving NBIC technologies,
- And to the shorter-term lead-up to the Singularity, as AI gains more general capabilities.

In both cases, *anticipation and management* of possible outcomes will be of vital importance.

By the way – in case it's not already clear – please don't expect a clever novel piece of technology, or some brilliant technical design, to somehow solve, by itself, the challenges posed by NBIC technologies and AGI. These challenges extend far beyond what could be wrestled into submission by some dazzling mathematical wizardry, by the incorporation of an ingenious new piece of silicon at the heart of every computer, or by any other "quick fix". Indeed, the considerable effort being invested by some organisations in a search for that kind of fix is, arguably, a distraction from a sober assessment of the bigger picture.

Better technology, better product design, better mathematics, and better hardware can all be *part* of the full solution. But that full solution also needs, critically, to include aspects of organisational design, economic incentives, legal frameworks, and political oversight. That's the argument I develop in the chapters ahead.

Collective insight

It has been my privilege and pleasure to be the person who has committed these principles into writing. However, the ideas in this book have benefitted greatly from the collective insight of the London Futurists community[4], as well as from feedback from people who have read my previous books[5], commented on my blogposts[6], or attended some of my speaking engagements[7].

In particular, I gratefully acknowledge diverse inputs over the years from numerous:

- Scientists, technologists, and engineers
- Entrepreneurs, designers, and artists
- Humanitarians, activists, and lawyers
- Educators, psychologists, and economists
- Philosophers, rationalists, and effective altruists
- Historians, sociologists, and forecasters
- Ethicists, transhumanists, and singularitarians.

I stand on the shoulders of all these contributors.

It is my sincere hope that this kind of collective insight can deepen and accelerate, and that this book can play a vital role in that process.

As a result, the 2020s can transform from *the Decade of Confusion* into *the Decade of Clarity, Choice, and Creativity*.

But if that collective insight fails to rise to the occasion, the 2020s and/or the 2030s could become, instead, *the Decade of Cataclysm*. The forces involved are that strong.

The short form of the Principles

Here's the short form of the Singularity Principles.

As we develop and interact with increasingly powerful technologies, we should be sure we understand:

1. *The goals that we're hoping to accomplish – rather than us merely drifting along in some direction because it sounds nice, or has some alluring features, or it seemed like a good idea the last time that we thought about strategic direction*
2. *What are the products and methods that are most likely to serve these goals well – rather than us persisting with products or methods that happen to make us feel comfortable, or which have given us some good results in the past*
3. *How we will manage the surprises arising en route to our goals – rather than us being caught flat-footed as the victim of inertia or denial, when unexpected signals start showing on our radars.*

These are important high-level points. But we need to dig deeper into how to apply them. That's what's covered in the pages ahead.

The four areas covered by the Principles

The Singularity Principles split into four areas:

1. Methods to analyse the goals and outcomes that may arise from particular technologies
2. The characteristics that are highly desirable in technological solutions
3. Methods to ensure that development takes place responsibly
4. Evolution and enforcement:
   - How this overall set of recommendations will evolve further over time
   - How to increase the likelihood that these recommendations are applied in practice rather than simply being some kind of wishful thinking.

I've given the principles in each of these four areas the following names:

- Analysing goals and potential outcomes:
  - *Question desirability*
  - *Clarify externalities*
  - *Require peer reviews*
  - *Involve multiple perspectives*
  - *Analyse the whole system*
  - *Anticipate fat tails*
- Desirable characteristics of tech solutions:
  - *Reject opacity*
  - *Promote resilience*
  - *Promote verifiability*
  - *Promote auditability*
  - *Clarify risks to users*
  - *Clarify trade-offs*
- Ensuring development takes place responsibly:

- *Insist on accountability*
    - *Penalise disinformation*
    - *Design for cooperation*
    - *Analyse via simulations*
    - *Maintain human oversight*
- Evolution and enforcement:
    - *Build consensus regarding principles*
    - *Provide incentives to address omissions*
    - *Halt development if principles not upheld*
    - *Consolidate progress via legal frameworks*

That makes 21 principles in total. We'll spend some time in the middle portion of this book on each of them in turn.

But first, the next few chapters will provide context, to help raise awareness of how and why all of us, in our own ways, should become active supporters of these principles.

1. Ten essential observations

The Singularity Principles arise from a number of general observations. These observations make it essential that we improve our collective abilities to anticipate and manage disruptive changes, *before an acceleration and intensification of such changes undermine the conditions for human flourishing*.

Tech breakthroughs are unpredictable (both timing and impact)

History teaches us that breakthroughs in technological capability may be dramatic and unexpected. That's both in terms of *timing* (such as an explosive breakthrough following a long period of disappointingly slow progress) and in terms of *impact* (with some breakthroughs being more widely applicable than was previously anticipated).

Some critics assert that, on the contrary, we can be sure that technological capability is reaching a plateau. They claim that all the low-hanging fruit have been picked.

To counter this counter, observe that:

- There is no fixed scientific barrier that would prevent further improvements in, for example, nanotech, biotech, infotech, or cognotech. As Nobel Physics laureate Richard Feynman once said, "There is plenty of room at the bottom"[8]
- More engineers and entrepreneurs than ever before have been trained in a rich variety of methods to develop new technologies, including methods both for incremental improvement and for the creation of disruptive new platforms

- The tools and resources available to help develop new technology have unprecedented capability.

Potential complex interactions make prediction even harder

Surprise interactions between overlapping developments in different fields can make outcomes even harder to predict.

These parallel changes include apparently unrelated technological transitions, disruptive breakthroughs as well as incremental progress, and changes in tooling, in prevailing open standards, and the quality of training data.

These overlapping changes also include updates in legal systems, popular culture, and general philosophical zeitgeist. That takes us to the next observation.

Changes in human attributes complicate tech changes

In anticipating future scenarios, it's a mistake to treat human institutions, human attitudes, and human intentions as fixed and unchangeable. Changes in all these aspects of the human outlook can be part of a complex network of responses to technological risks and opportunities.

It is as renowned management consultant Peter Drucker observed, "the major questions regarding technology are not technical but human questions"[9].

For example, education and training can smooth the path of swift transition and safe adoption. Carefully targeted government subsidies can play a role too. The storylines in popular Netflix dramas can trigger positive changes in attitude in the general public toward products featuring helpful new capabilities. And so on.

On the other hand, changes in human institutions, attitudes, and intentions can also make matters worse. Unhelpful new trade barriers can hinder the adoption of safer technologies. Clumsy changes in regulations can lead to the faster spread of dangerous technologies. Public sentiment can be transformed by fast-spreading misinformation. And there can be an escalating copycat response to publicity stunts from media stars that irresponsibly endorse – or oppose – specific new products.

Accordingly, forecasts of the impacts of technologies – whether beneficial or destructive – will likely be misleading unless they consider the two-way interactions between human changes and technological changes.

Greater tech power enables more devastating results

The more powerful technology becomes, the more devastating are the results it can produce – including devastatingly *good* results and devastatingly *bad* results.

Some examples:

- Small fireworks with errant trajectories can, in some cases, ignite a conflagration that causes widespread damage. But larger explosives, such as nuclear bombs, can destroy an entire city in the blink of an eye.
- Documents individually hand-copied by scribes spread ideas gradually for centuries, but Gutenberg's printing presses placed books and pamphlets into many more hands, accelerating the Renaissance and the Reformation, and triggering decades of turmoil all over Europe.

- The flow of disinformation has caused problems throughout human history, but with modern online social networks spanning billions of users, disinformation nowadays travels at the speed of light, and has sparked near genocide[10].

Different perspectives assess "good" vs. "bad" differently

Results that are evaluated as "good" from one perspective, such as an increase in profits or in market share, or breaking records for speed or performance, can also be evaluated as "bad" from other perspectives – for example when externalities are included in calculations, or when a broader view of human flourishing is considered.

Competition can be hazardous as well as beneficial

Although a competitive marketplace can often accelerate positive progress, with companies racing to discover and apply useful new innovations, such competition can also result in dangerous corner-cutting or other reckless risk-taking. Hostile arms races are particularly hazardous.

Indeed, a strong competitive environment makes forecasting the future all the more difficult:

- If two or more competitors perceive that a decisive gain will be attained by the first group to develop some new technology, they will work harder to win that race
- If two or more competitors perceive that *other groups* are striving hard to gain a key advantage, they will be inclined *to redouble their own efforts*

- In a fiercely competitive environment, groups will be inclined to keep some of their interim progress a secret, and also to spread FUD (fear, uncertainty, and doubt) to distract observers from a clear understanding of what is actually happening.

Some tech failures would be too drastic to allow recovery

Although there are many technological failures from which it's possible to recover, with people (hopefully) growing wiser as a result, some technological failures may have such a vast scale that subsequent recovery would be extremely hard or even impossible. In these cases, there's no hope for "failing forward" or "failing smart". The only option in such cases is to avoid failures in the first place.

The more powerful the underlying technology, the more attention needs to be paid to such possibilities.

A history of good results is no guarantee of future success

The mere fact that a piece of technology has delivered a string of good results in the past does not guarantee, by itself, that the technology in question will deliver good results in altered circumstances in the future. Previous methods may fail, for unexpected reasons, when parts of the overall system are different from in the past.

The management of technological change therefore needs to rely on more than what philosophers call "induction", that is, the assumption (implicit or explicit) that the future will continue to resemble the past.

It's insufficient to rely on good intentions

Something else that it's insufficient to rely on is the perceived *good intentions* of individuals or companies – intentions that these individuals or companies will avoid any very bad outcomes. Alas, when good intentions are coupled with a mistaken or incomplete understanding of an issue, they can result in the very sort of bad outcomes they were seeking to avoid. Moreover, these good intentions can sometimes lose their strength, being submerged under other forces that are more powerful.

Wishful thinking predisposes blindness to problems

Due to wishful thinking, providers of potential new technological solutions are often inclined to turn a blind eye to problematic features that may arise. If they hear reports of adverse side-effects or possible unintended consequences, they are motivated to disbelieve these reports, or to distort them or throw doubt on them.

They won't just seek to deceive the general public. They'll even seek to deceive themselves, in order to sound and appear more convincing when they issue their denials.

American writer Upton Sinclair said it well in 1935: "It is difficult to get a man to understand something, when his salary depends upon his not understanding it!"[11]

That's another reason why greater vigilance is needed, and why openness and transparency should be rewarded.

Taken together, the above ten observations underscore the need to go beyond mere wishful thinking.

Next, let's explore more concretely the set of risks and benefits that may arise from fast-changing technologies.

2. Fast-changing technologies: risks and benefits

Let's start with some good news. Technologies have provided many huge benefits to humanity:

- Better health, via better medical treatments, better hygiene, and better nutrition
- More knowledge created and shared
- Greater availability of labour-saving devices
- Ability to travel more widely and have richer experiences.

However, it's also the case that technologies are prone to have side-effects that are unforeseen and unwelcome:

- Drugs to treat medical conditions can have side-effects that are worse than the original sickness – an example being thalidomide, which caused horrific birth defects[12]
- Widespread use of antibiotic drugs can stimulate the emergence of bacteria that are resistant to these drugs, threatening the spread of an untreatable infection[13]
- Chemicals intended to control insects that carry diseases can damage other parts of the environment – an example being the insecticide DDT[14]
- Chemicals added into industrial processes to boost performance or increase strength can have unexpected detrimental effects on the health of people in the vicinity – examples being lead

(added to petrol)[15] and asbestos (used in buildings)[16]
- CFC chemicals used in refrigeration and in aerosols migrated high into the stratosphere, where they destabilised ozone molecules, allowing larger quantities of harmful UV radiation from the sun to reach the earth's surface, increasing incidents of skin cancer[17]
- A hydroelectric dam can generate significant quantities of electricity, but if the dam wall breaks, enormous damage can result[18] to the people and habitat in the path of the water that rushes out; similar concerns apply to nuclear power stations with inadequate safety measures[19]
- Innovative financial assets, such as Credit Default Swaps, Collateralised Debt Obligations, and other so-called credit derivatives, that can enable more investment in particular areas, can also destabilise financial markets, earning themselves the disparaging description "financial weapons of mass destruction"[20]

That brings us to the 64 trillion-dollar question:

How can the balance of risks and benefits be moved away from risks and toward greater benefits?

Technology risk factors

Other things being equal, a piece of technology is liable to cause more damage:
- If it is deployed at larger scale – for example, a larger hydroelectric dam may cause greater

damage, if the dam wall breaks, than a smaller dam
- If it is deployed more widely – a chemical used throughout the world may have more drastic side-effects than a chemical used in just one location
- If it embodies more power – for example, high voltage electricity lines that are blown out of their intended routing may result in a more damaging discharge than low voltage lines
- If their method of operation is obscure and poorly understood – increasing the chance that they will operate in unexpected ways in subtly changed circumstances
- If the people or systems overseeing these technologies pay less attention, or lack adequate training or incentives to perform their tasks well
- If the people or systems overseeing these technologies cover up or downplay evidence of problems with the technology, and harass or ridicule people who want to highlight such evidence.

The above conditions can be called "technology risk factors".

Unfortunately, several of these risk factors are likely to be *increased* when a new technology shows a lot of promise, and its backers are keen to take fuller advantage of it. In such a case, the backers would prefer:

- To deploy the technology at larger scale, and more widely, so that it can reach more people
- To run the technology at higher power, so that it is more likely to achieve striking results

- To minimise attention to any evidence of apparent behaviour that could cause the technology to be withdrawn.

Other risk factors will increase if the technology is complex and fast-changing:

- Its operating principles are less likely to be understood
- The people overseeing the technology are less likely to be adequately trained in all aspects of its operation.

There's an additional set of complications when technology is changing quickly:

- An assessment of risks associated with the technology could become invalidated, due to the greater capabilities acquired in a subsequent version of the technology
- If the first group to develop that technology could gain a significant advantage, commercially or geopolitically, there will be incentives to cut corners with the implementation of safety measures, in a rush to obtain "first mover advantage"
- Fast-changing technology can alter, not only the primary solution being developed, but also the environment in which that solution operates, making reliable foresight harder.

Prioritising benefits?

One approach to the risk-benefit balance is to focus more on the benefits than the risks:

- Rather than slowing down the development and deployment of technology, from fear of damage arising, the priority would be *to accelerate that development and deployment*, in order to achieve the envisioned benefits more quickly
- Any unexpected and unwelcome side-effects can, in this approach, be addressed as and when they arise
- Responses to these side-effects will in any case be a valuable part of learning; any apparent "technology failures" can assist in faster acquisition of knowledge (about what works and what doesn't work).

This approach – which is sometimes described as "techno-optimistic" – might be seen as especially attractive if the potential benefits from the new technology have huge scale:

- Large numbers of lives could be saved, by innovative new treatments for cancer, dementia, and so on
- New nuclear power plants could generate enormous quantities of green energy, allowing faster reduction of emissions of greenhouse gases
- Geoengineering interventions in the stratosphere – or by changing the composition of the oceans – could reverse the dangerous trend toward excessively high global temperatures
- AI algorithms with greater general intelligence could propose profound novel solutions to longstanding issues of healthcare, global warming,

and the management of the financial and economic markets.

Techno-optimists urge, accordingly, a speed-up in the development and deployment of breakthrough innovative technologies.

The problem, nevertheless, is that any technology with greater potential to deliver profound benefits has, at the same time, greater potential for disastrous unexpected side-effects. Recall, again, the metaphor of the two-edged sword.

By itself, this is no reason to try to slow down the development and deployment of new technology. However, it *is* a reason to ramp up *parallel* efforts to anticipate and manage any side-effects that may arise.

Such efforts can be guided by the principles described in the pages ahead.

What about ethics?

The development and deployment of technologies is sometimes addressed from the viewpoint of ethics. Thus it is common to hear advocacy for "the ethical use of technology", or, more simply, for "AI ethics".

This framing can cause problems. Self-proclaimed ethicists are sometimes perceived as dour, unimaginative people who mainly say "no", as in "thou shalt not do this" and "thou shalt not do that". Understandably, technologists and entrepreneurs sometimes bristle, when they perceive that they are being upbraided by critics whose ideas appear to derive from contentious philosophical or theological worldviews. The technologists and entrepreneurs want to proceed with the task, as they see it, of building a significantly better world. They're disinterested in interference from apparent do-gooders.

Moreover, the common ethical injunctions to ensure "fair" or "equitable" access to technologies are subject to controversy as well, since there are divergent views on what counts as "fair" and "equitable". Just banging the table and saying "this needs to be more fair" is only the very beginning of a complex discussion.

Nevertheless, the Singularity Principles do endorse one of the fundamental insights of ethics:

- Just because we believe we *could* develop some technology, and even if we feel some *desires* to develop that technology, that's not a *sufficient* reason for us actually to go ahead and develop it and deploy it.

More briefly: *could* does not imply *should*.

However, the Singularity Principles take as their starting point an appeal, not to any elaborate ethical framework, but to considerations of potential harm and potential benefit – especially considerations of potential *catastrophic* harm or potential *profound* benefit.

It's far from easy to calculate in advance the likely impacts of various technology projects on catastrophic harm or profound benefit. That's where the guidelines of the Singularity Principles come to the fore. They provide a number of short-cut recommendations of the form, "It's *generally* good to do this" or "It's *generally* bad to do that". Whether you agree with these recommendations may depend on your assessment of the extent that, on the whole, they will indeed alter the likelihood of catastrophic harm or profound benefit.

2. Fast-changing technologies: risks and benefits

The transhumanist stance

I'll insert here one additional quick comment on the subject of ethics. Answers to the question "what *should* we do" generally presuppose a view about which kinds of state of being are more *virtuous*.

One family of ethical views tends to regard the lives of certain people in the long-distant past as somehow the most virtuous. These people – such as founders and leading figures of religions – are said to provide role models for us to seek to emulate.

Another family of ethical views tends to look to elements of the present day, or the recent past, as models that the lifestyles of all people should attain.

The Singularity Principles make neither of these assumptions. Instead, they conform to what can be called "the transhumanist stance"[21] – the view that people in the future (including the near future) can attain levels of wellbeing, consciousness, and virtue, that radically surpass what has been attained at any previous period in history.

Transhumanists do not accept that our vision should be constrained by the accomplishments and achievements of the past. Transhumanists anticipate a dramatic uplift in human capability – an uplift in capability that will be available to everyone.

What will enable that uplift is wise application of the possibilities provided by new technology – technologies that can significantly improve:

- Health, longevity, and resilience
- Intelligence, insight, and awareness
- Collaboration and creativity

- Sustainable living
- Mental and emotional wellbeing.

In short, the transhumanist stance is that it is possible, and desirable, to significantly improve all aspects of human life, by the wise application of science and technology, guided by clear thinking[22].

From this point of view, it would be *doubly* tragic if emerging fast-changing technologies were mismanaged. The first tragedy is the civilisational collapse that is likely to ensue. The second tragedy is humanity being prevented from reaching the much higher levels of flourishing that were so close to being attained.

Moving forward

The technology risk factors discussed above – and the range of benefits that technology can enable – apply to a wide spread of different technologies. Next, let's consider how this picture changes when we focus on one particular technology, namely artificial intelligence.

2.1 Special complications with AI

The principles to best govern the rise of artificial intelligence (AI) are a natural extension of the general set of principles covered in this book.

However, a number of special characteristics of AI deserve particular attention. These split into two groups:

1. Special characteristics of AI *as it already exists*
   - Problems with training data
   - Black-box nature
   - Interactions between multiple algorithms
2. Special characteristics that AI *can be expected to acquire in the future*
   - Self-improving AI
   - Devious AI
   - Potential catastrophic disaster

Problems with training data

Today's AI often involves complex statistical models that have been "trained" – configured – by reference to large sets of "training data". For example, this data could include:

- Photographs of faces
- Sets of translations of text – such as are produced by official (human) translators working for multinational organisations
- Recordings of text spoken with different accents

2.1 Special complications with AI

- Archives of games of chess, as played by human experts
- General collections of photographs found on the Internet.

On some occasions, this data is "labelled", meaning that a description is provided along with the item of data. On other occasions, the data lacks labels, but the training algorithm infers patterns and groupings by itself.

Three kinds of problems can arise:

First, the data might incorporate unwelcome biases:

- It might reflect "historical reality" (in which fewer members of some demographics attained various positions in society) rather than "desired reality"
- It might under-represent various segments of society; for example, photographs of hands might only include people with certain skin colours
- It might over-represent various patterns of usage, such as the modes of language used by official translators, rather than more slang usage.

Second, even if the data has no unwelcome biases, an algorithm might fail to learn it fully; it might give acceptable answers on the majority of occasions, but a grossly incorrect answer on other occasions. (This problem is linked to the "black box" nature of the algorithms used, as discussed later in this chapter.)

Third, even if an algorithm performs excellently on examples that conform to the same patterns and formats as the training data, it may give abhorrent answers when presented with "out-of-distribution" examples. Such examples might include:

- Pictures with different orientation
- Voice samples spoken in different accents
- Pictures that have been subtly altered – for example, by the addition of small marks.

Two issues with out-of-distribution examples deserve particular attention:

1. Some examples might be deliberately altered, by agents with hostile intent, in order to mislead the algorithm; these are known as "adversarial" cases
2. It's by no means obvious, in advance, what are the limits of the distribution on which the algorithm has been trained, and which subtle changes will throw it off course.

The black box nature of AI

In principle, many of the above issues can be solved if an AI system offers a clear explanation of its reasons for particular decisions.

Thus instead of just saying "this medical scan probably contains evidence of a malignant tumour: urgent surgery is recommended", the AI system should indicate:

- The features of the medical scan it used in reaching its conclusion
- The features of the training data which back up the conclusion reached
- Any contrary indications that should also be borne in mind.

Again, instead of just saying "the CV of this candidate means they are a comparatively poor fit for a specific job vacancy", the AI system should indicate:

2.1 Special complications with AI

- The features of the CV it used in reaching its conclusion
- The features of the training data which back up the conclusion reached
- Any contrary indications that should also be borne in mind.

However, in practice there are many situations where no such clear explanation of the decisions made by an AI algorithm can be offered. Instead, an analysis of the internal state of the statistical model (the multiple layers of "software neurons") used by the AI system will yield only a vast collection of numbers. The scale of these numbers means they defy any simple explanations.

The operations of the algorithm may as well be a "black box", with no visibility as to what is happening inside.

Interactions between multiple algorithms

A third complicating factor with present-day AI systems is an extension of the point previously noted, whereby a system can produce surprisingly wrong results in circumstances that differ from those typical of the training set used to configure the algorithm.

In this case, the new feature of the environment is an unexpected new AI system, which coexists with the first one. The new system might be altering aspects of the landscape in which the first system operates:

- It might do so in an adversarial manner, with an intent to alter the behaviour of the first system

- Alternatively, its operations may simply overlap with that of the first system, without any intentional manipulation.

In other words, two different AI systems can interact with each other to create a new category of risks, different from the risks that either of the systems might generate in isolation.

For an amusing real-life example, consider the interaction of two simple algorithms, each of which adjusted the price at which a book would be offered for sale, based on the price offered by a competing online bookseller[23]:

- One bookseller, profnath, periodically set the price of the book to be 0.9983 times the price quoted by the other bookseller, bordeebook
- Bordeebook, independently, periodically adjusted the price of the book to be 1.270589 times the price quoted by profnath
- The booksellers each had their own reasons for making these adjustments, in line with their brand positioning or sales strategy
- The result, however, was that one book ended up being listed for sale at the astronomical price of $23,698,655.93 per copy (plus, as it happens, $3.99 shipping).

That particular example was relatively harmless, but other interactions could be much more serious – especially if the algorithms involved were more complex.

Similar "combination effects" already exist with other technologies:

2.1 Special complications with AI

- Two or more drugs, treating different diseases in the same person, can interfere with each other
- Two or more agricultural innovations, addressing different crops growing in nearby environments, can interfere with each other
- Two or more geo-engineering interventions, each intended to reduce the effects of greenhouse gas emissions, could interfere with each other.

What's different in the case of two or more AI systems interacting is the ways in which the issues previously noted can combine:

- Two or more black box systems, whose internal operations cannot be usefully explained, can produce even bigger surprises when interfering with each other
- Two or more AI systems, that each view a data point as conforming to the basic parameters of their training data, have an increased chance that the data point will be out-of-distribution in at least one case
- Two or more AI systems, that each try to guard against possible biases within their training data, have an increased chance that unexpected biases will prevail in at least one case.

More significantly, the potential for surprise combination effects *grows* when we consider, not just AI systems with today's capabilities, but the more powerful AI systems that are likely to be developed in the future.

It's now time to review how these forthcoming AI systems will introduce yet more complications.

Self-improving AI

There already exist AI systems which can help with the design of other AI systems.

Consider the field of AutoML, that is, "automated machine learning". AutoML is described as follows[24]:

> Automated Machine Learning provides methods and processes to make Machine Learning available for non-Machine Learning experts, to improve efficiency of Machine Learning and to accelerate research on Machine Learning.

That description is from the website of the group of researchers who are investigating the possibilities of AutoML[25]. They note that the creation of successful ML models presently "crucially relies on human machine learning experts to perform" a number of tasks. These tasks include:

- Preprocessing and cleaning training data
- Selecting which kind of machine learning model is best suited to a particular task
- Selecting the so-called "model hyperparameters" which define the basic operating mode of the machine learning model
- Designing the connections between different layers of a potentially "deep" neural network
- Assessing the results obtained.

The AutoML researchers comment as follows:

> As the complexity of these tasks is often beyond non-ML-experts, the rapid growth of machine learning applications has created a demand for off-the-shelf machine learning methods that can be used easily and without expert knowledge. We call the resulting

2.1 SPECIAL COMPLICATIONS WITH AI

research area that targets progressive automation of machine learning *AutoML*.

In just a few short years, significant progress has been made with AutoML, both in academia and in industry. As early as 2017, Wired technology journalist Tom Simonite wrote a report with the headline "Google's Learning Software Learns to Write Learning Software"[26]. Here's an excerpt:

> In a project called AutoML, Google's researchers have taught machine-learning software to build machine-learning software. In some instances, what it comes up with is more powerful and efficient than the best systems the researchers themselves can design. Google says the system recently scored a record 82 percent at categorizing images by their content. On the harder task of marking the location of multiple objects in an image, an important task for augmented reality and autonomous robots, the auto-generated system scored 43 percent. The best human-built system scored 39 percent.

AutoML is an example of a larger trend within AI, namely the application of AI to solve engineering design problems. Examples of this trend include the use of AI:

- To monitor and improve the design of Formula One racing cars[27]
- To improve the design and layout of printed circuit boards (PCBs)[28]
- To accelerate the discovery and design of new pharmaceuticals[29]
- To design new communication and radar systems that are more resilient in congested environments[30].

As time progresses, AI systems will be poised to play, in a similar way, larger roles in the design and operation *of new AI systems*. This positive-feedback self-improvement loop could accelerate the emergence of more capable AI. But it also increases the risks of outcomes that are unforeseen and dangerous, especially when:

- There are competitive pressures to apply new design techniques as soon as possible
- The design systems appear to produce good results, but their own operation retains elements that are opaque (black box)
- Two or more AI systems, with incompletely understood interference effects, are involved in the design and operation of a next-generation system.

A latent defect in an original AI system, which causes no significant problem in an original implementation, could be magnified by a process of self-enhancement, to the point where the underlying problem has a *much* larger impact.

Devious AI

The problems arising from the black box nature of AI systems — when aspects of their internal operations are unable to be explained in any simple way — are magnified when an AI has an incentive to operate *deviously* — that is, to deliberately mislead some observers about aspects of its internal operations.

Deception has been a ubiquitous aspect of human minds since prehistoric times. We have many reasons to want to deceive each other — to gain advantages in terms of resources, position, community status, and so on. One reason the human brain grew substantially in power and capability during the long evolution of homo sapiens from primate ancestors was because of an arms race[31]:

- There were incentives to become more skilled in deceiving others
- There were also incentives to become more skilled in detecting and keeping track of deceptions (sometimes without it becoming known that we were aware of a deception).

For AI systems, the considerations are more subtle, but there remain reasons why an AI might seek to deceive other intelligent entities. This involves adversarial situations – or situations that could *become* adversarial. For example, an AI system that is aware that another intelligence might seek to hack it, or otherwise subvert it, might find it advantageous to misrepresent some of its capabilities and inner states. It might even wish to "play dead" – or to "play *dumb*".

A different kind of example is that of the so-called "white lie", when one intelligent being decides that it is in the best interests of another intelligent being to hear a mistruth – a "white lie".

The complication is that, the greater the intelligence of an AI system, the greater is its ability to deceive various observers. Being smarter means you can be more devious.

Four catastrophic error modes

The end outcome of the various trends noted above is that an AI system may acquire so much influence over human society and our surrounding environment, that a mistake in that system could cataclysmically reduce human wellbeing all over the world. Billions of lives could be extinguished, or turned into a very pale reflection of their present state.

Such an outcome could arise in any of four ways – four catastrophic error modes. In brief, these are:

1. Defect in implementation
2. Defect in design
3. Design overridden
4. Implementation overridden.

In more detail:

1. The system contains a defect in its implementation. It takes an action that it calculates will have one outcome, but, disastrously, it has another outcome instead. For example, a geo-engineering intervention could trigger an unforeseen change in the global climate, plunging the earth into a state in which humans cannot survive.
2. The system contains a defect in its design. It takes actions to advance the goals it has *explicitly* been given, but does so in a way that catastrophically reduces actual human wellbeing. For example, a clumsily specified goal to *focus on preserving the diversity of the earth's biosystem* could be met by eliminating upward of 99% of all humans.
3. The system has been given goals that are well aligned with human wellbeing, but as the system evolves, a different set of goals emerge, in which the wellbeing of humans is deprioritised. This is similar to the way in which the recent emergence of higher thinking capabilities in human primates led to many humans taking actions in opposition

to the gene-spreading instincts placed into our biology by evolution.

4. The system has been given goals that are well aligned with human wellbeing, but the system is reconfigured by hackers of one sort or another – perhaps from malevolence, or perhaps from a misguided sense that various changes would make the system more powerful (and hence more valuable).

Some critics suggest that it will be relatively easy to avoid these four catastrophic error modes. The next three chapters provide arguments that, on the contrary, these error modes are deeply problematic. These chapters are:

- "The Control Problem"
- "The Alignment Problem"
- "No easy solutions".

The chapters after that will describe in some depth the principles which *can* provide solutions, namely the Singularity Principles.

The broader perspective

Note that adherence to the Singularity Principles won't just reduce the risks of catastrophic error. Importantly, that adherence will also reduce the occurrences of errors that, whilst not catastrophic on a global scale, still result in significant harm to human potential – harming people by denying them opportunity, crippling them, or (in, alas, too many cases) killing them.

Moreover, adherence to these principles won't just reduce the chances of harm arising from errors with AI. It will also reduce the chances of harm arising from errors with other types of technology, such as NBIC.

Finally, the Singularity Principles aren't just about avoiding significant harm. Critically, they're also about raising the probability of attaining profound benefits.

But we won't obtain these benefits unless we solve the issues of control and/or alignment. So let's next look at these issues in more depth.

2.2 The AI Control Problem

How does a physically weaker species keep control of members of physically stronger species?

For example, how do humans avoid being overwhelmed by gorillas, by elephants, or by tigers?

Three answers:

1. By taking advantage of technologies, such as spears, tranquiliser guns, and specially built enclosures
2. By strength of numbers, with individual humans grouping together to boost their defensive capabilities
3. By raw cunning, in order to outwit the planning of the physically stronger animals.

But what if new creatures exceed human capabilities, not only in physical strength, but also in intelligence? How would we avoid being overwhelmed in such a case?

That's the challenge posed by the AI Control Problem – which is sometimes also called "the gorilla problem".

The gorilla problem

The term "gorilla problem" was introduced by AI researcher Stuart Russell, a professor at Berkeley[32]:

> It doesn't require much imagination to see that making something smarter than yourself could be a bad idea. We understand that our control over our environment and over other species is a result of our intelligence, so the thought of something else being more intelligent

than us – whether it's a robot or an alien – immediately induces a queasy feeling.

Around ten million years ago, the ancestors of the modern gorilla created (accidentally, to be sure) the genetic lineage leading to modern humans. How do the gorillas feel about this? Clearly, if they were able to tell us about their species' current situation vis-à-vis humans, the consensus opinion would be very negative indeed. Their species has essentially no future beyond that which we deign to allow.

We do not want to be in a similar situation vis-à-vis superintelligent machines. I'll call this *the gorilla problem* – specifically, the problem of whether humans can maintain their supremacy and autonomy in a world that includes machines with substantially greater intelligence.

The risks to humans in such a world can be classified into the four catastrophic error modes already mentioned:

1. **Defect in implementation**: The superintelligence is by no means infallible: it takes an action which is intended to progress a goal, but due to an error in calculation (or an error in execution) a sudden disastrous outcome ensues
2. **Defect in design**: The superintelligence pursues goals originally designed into it by humans, but pursues these goals in a way neither foreseen nor intended by humans, resulting – again – in an outcome that is disastrous for human wellbeing
3. **Design overridden**: New goals or targets emerge, either within the superintelligence itself, or within a larger system in which the superintelligence exists, that no longer put a priority on human wellbeing (a bit like how humans don't particularly

prioritise supporting eight billion gorillas living on the planet)
4. **Implementation overridden**: The superintelligence is hacked, or reconfigured, in ways that violate its original goals, and its subsequent actions have a terrible impact on humanity.

In all four of these cases, human observers may realise, for a period of time, that something is going catastrophically wrong, but due to the greater power and greater cunning possessed by the superintelligence, this realisation will do nothing to hinder the outcome.

Examples of dangers with uncontrollable AI

Consider some examples of the dangers posed by uncontrollable AI.

Automated systems already play various roles in the oversight and management of a number of weapons systems. At present, decisions taken by these systems are generally subject to real-time review and approval by humans. However, new threats are posed by the introduction of cruise missiles that can travel at hypersonic speeds – at 20 times the speed of sound, namely, four miles per second. This increased speed reduces the amount of time between the detection of a possible incoming attack, and the launch of any defensive measures (anti-missile missiles). Accordingly, the pressure increases to remove the requirements for humans to consider and approve the launch of such counter-measures.

In principle, defensive measures could be launched in a hurry, with the possibility of being recalled after their launch in case humans determine that the situation is a

2.2 THE AI CONTROL PROBLEM

false alarm. However, any such real-time control over defence missiles is potentially vulnerable to hacking: messages to disengage could be sent from an attacker, spuriously, rather than from the defender. To guard against such misdirection, additional layers of security may be introduced inside the defence systems.

However, a combination of errors could have terrible consequences – somewhat similar to the scenario depicted as long ago as the 1964 film *Dr Strangelove*[33]:

- Missiles could be launched for defensive reasons, even though no actual attack was incoming
- Once launched, these purportedly defensive missiles might resist all attempts to switch them off, due to flaws in their security system
- Instead of striking incoming missiles, these purportedly defensive missiles could detonate in ways that inflict large damage on civilian infrastructure
- Other automated systems could inflict yet more damage in reaction to this first wave of destruction.

For a second example, consider AI systems that automate, not the launch of military weapons, but the rapid buying or selling of financial assets. Two or more of these systems could interact in a way that destabilises the entire global financial system. Such interactions are believed to lie at the root of various controversial "flash crash" episodes[34] in which, so far, the damage has been relatively localised. However, there is no guarantee that future recurrences will likewise have only limited impact.

Third, consider the various shadowy institutions (often with three-letter names) that design malware with the intent to spy on the systems of enemy countries or to damage the systems these enemies are creating. As described in the book *This Is How They Tell Me the World Ends: The Cyberweapons Arms Race*[35] by New York Times reporter Nicole Perlroth, this malware often takes devastating advantage of obscure flaws inside software platforms such as Microsoft Windows. This malware is sometimes surprisingly sophisticated, relying on multiple software defects and communications between several parts of an extended system. With additional AI capabilities, that malware could become more adept in the pursuit of its goals. However, malware systems have a history of being hijacked, duplicated, or reverse-engineered, by the very people that the initial institutes wanted to monitor and control. Moreover, altered versions of the malware can go on to inflict wide, indiscriminate damage, in ways that are increasingly hard to prevent.

Fourth, consider a company that develops an AI system with powerful new capabilities, and which deploys this AI to create and issue messages on social media that stimulate consumers to purchase services from the company. These messages might vary on account of recent events reported in the news, so that they appear particularly relevant. As revenues soar, the company may be encouraged to give that AI system more autonomy, rather than slowing down its performance with human reviews of all its proposals. But then, roughly as happened with the Tay chatbot released by Microsoft in 2016[36], some of the messages could contain unexpected material that provokes a severe backlash. Enraged observers might initiate hostile measures in response to these extreme communications.

Similar examples could be considered that involve AI systems mismanaging aspects of:

- The global climate – using geoengineering capabilities
- Food production – using novel fertilisers, genetically modified crops, or other interventions in the environment
- Responses to a new infectious pandemic – using measures intended to stop the spread of that infection, similar to the way that a rapidly created firebreak is intended to stop the spread of an oncoming mass forest fire
- The removal of microplastics from the environment – introducing new chemical elements which, nevertheless, have unexpected side-effects of their own.

Alongside the examples that we are able to foresee, we also need to bear in mind "unknown unknowns", where AI is applied in ways that we cannot yet anticipate, but which may appear to make good sense once new capabilities have been developed. These new AI capabilities may introduce unknown error modes of their own.

The complication is that, as AI becomes more powerful, and is in consequence more capable of generating hugely beneficial outcomes, there will be more pressure to deploy it – even though it will also, by virtue of its greater power, be more capable of generating deeply disastrous outcomes.

Proposed solutions (which don't work)

When people first hear about the AI control problem, they often remark that there are straightforward ways to solve that problem. The solutions they present include the following:

1. Require that the operation of the AI has been fully verified beforehand, so that no bugs can be present
2. Avoid giving the AI any incentive ("emotion" or "volition") that might cause it to take actions detrimental to humans
3. Ensure that the AI can be turned off
4. Arrange for tripwires to close down the AI in the event that it acts in violation of previously identified limits
5. Restrict the AI to operate at arm's length from the real world, confined in a so-called "box"
6. Restrict the resources which are at the disposal of the AI, and/or its possible operating parameters, in order to keep it under human control
7. Rely on the good intelligence of the AI to automatically take actions in support of human wellbeing
8. Hardwire into the AI an unalterable prioritisation for human wellbeing, somewhat similar to Asimov's (fictional) Laws of Robotics.

However, as will now be reviewed, each of these intended solutions faces significant problems.

Note: other so-called "solutions" are equally common – and equally predictable. AI safety researcher Leo Gao has created what he calls a "Bad Alignment Take Bingo" card, which you can find online[37]. Rob Bensinger, another AI safety researcher, has produced a useful Twitter thread[38] in which he explains at some length why each of these "takes" are, indeed, "bad".

The impossibility of full verification

It's in the nature of a complex software system that any verification of its soundness can be at best provisional.

One reason for this is because any methods used to verify the soundness of the software could themselves have defects or limitations. Test frameworks could have blind spots. Logic checkers could be misled by certain unusual constructions. Code that is verified as being sound could be modified as the system runs, into a form that is no longer valid. And so on.

A second reason is more technical. It involves a discovery made in 1936 by computer science pioneer Alan Turing, in connection with what has become known as the "halting problem"[39]. Namely, for any software system with general capabilities, there are particular questions that it is not possible to determine, in advance, whether the system will ever reach a definite conclusion (that is, "halt"). In other words, the behaviour of the system contains some intrinsically unpredictable elements, and the outcome cannot always be verified in advance.

A third reason is that, even if software could be verified as conforming in all cases to the specification (design) laid down for it, there's still the possibility that the specification has failed to consider all eventualities.

To be clear, none of these reasons mean that attempts should be abandoned to verify the performance of an AI system before it is released. Indeed, the Singularity Principle "Promote verifiability" highlights the importance of such attempts.

Nevertheless, these attempts cannot, by themselves, guarantee that the software will always have beneficial outcomes. Accordingly, the principle of "Promote verifiability" can be only part of the overall solution.

Emotion misses the point

Can the risks of bad outcomes from AI be countered by means of avoiding giving the AI anything corresponding to the emotional drives of humans? After all, many of the destructive actions committed by humans arise from emotions such as spite, greed, resentment, and a raw will to power.

A similar idea is to avoid giving the AI anything corresponding to sentience or consciousness – elements which might cause the AI to take its own decisions, contrary to the instructions it has received from its programming.

But these ideas fail to appreciate that errors from AI systems often arise from the straightforward application of logic, and have nothing to do with either emotions or sentience.

Consider again the errors in the above examples involving weapons systems, financial systems, intelligent malware, communications on social media, geoengineering interventions, food production, disease prevention, and environmental restoration. The causes of these disasters have nothing to do with the AI system somehow gaining sentience, consciousness, or emotional feelings.

(In some cases, the AI system takes advantage of its *rational understanding* of human emotional responses – as in the example of manipulating social media. An AI could also *simulate* having emotions, by presenting a smiley face. But these are different matters from the AI *actually possessing* emotions of its own.)

As for the idea of avoiding designing an AI that has something akin to a "will to power", that's a more subtle topic. It turns out that the acquisition of more power naturally emerges as a subsidiary goal for AIs with a given level of general capability. The concept of the emergence of subsidiary goals is sometimes called "AI drives"[40].

Here's an analogy: individual humans can vary widely in terms of the goals they deem to be most important. But in nearly all cases, these humans recognise that their goals are likely to be advanced if they have access to more money. Money can purchase many resources that could bring their goals closer to fruition. For example, money can purchase better healthcare, or better security, or better education, or better travel, or better contractors – all of which could support whatever end goal the particular person has in mind. Therefore, despite the differences in end-goal, different people are likely to share a common subsidiary goal of having sufficient access to money.

In the same way, a rational AI with a given set of goals will recognise that it will be more likely to achieve these goals if it:

- Has access to more resources (such as more memory storage, more processing power, and faster communications networks)

- Has greater rationality – so that it can reason more effectively
- Has greater security – to prevent itself being undermined, thereby frustrating the pursuit of its goals
- Cannot be switched off – since it cannot fulfil its goals if it no longer exists
- Cannot have its objectives altered – since, again, it cannot fulfil its original goals if these goals are subsequently overridden.

Accordingly, even an AI without the slightest shade of internal emotion will start to take actions that defend its own autonomy and increase its access to useful resources.

No off switch

Present day computers can be switched off. So won't future AIs likewise have an off switch?

There are at least five problems with that line of thinking.

First, complex software systems exist in distributed forms, spread over multiple computers with multiple power supplies. There's no one electric switch that would turn off the entire Google search engine, the Facebook network, or the Bitcoin cryptocurrency.

Second, even if centralised electrical power were disabled, the software is likely to be running on systems with access to local power sources.

Third, any attempts to shut down all relevant electrical power systems will themselves have huge side-effects, such as preventing the operations of many other vital aspects of civilisation: transport, entertainment, food production, healthcare, defence, and so on. Accordingly, there will be strong resistance to any such attempts.

Fourth, an intelligent AI system will be motivated to "play dead" rather than actually be switched off. It may remain in a dormant state before unexpectedly springing back into animation, to finish whatever course of action it was previously pursuing.

Fifth, awareness of the need to terminate an AI system may arise too late, leaving humans too little time to respond. Humans might already be incapacitated by that time, like the proverbial frog in water that has slowly boiled. Ahead of the time when it has become apparent that the AI is going disastrously wrong, it may well be hailed by observers as operating brilliantly.

The ineffectiveness of tripwires

To guard against the possibility that humans won't be able to act fast enough, and comprehensively enough, to switch off an AI system that is noticed to be malfunctioning, what about the idea of introducing some internal tripwires?

If the AI is detected to be exceeding certain parameters, these tripwires could intervene, to disable the AI.

This would be similar to the "dead man's switch" for some train drivers. The driver had to keep a handle pressed down. In case the driver became incapacitated, the handle would spring open, and the train would automatically slow down and stop.

The idea has considerable merit. It features in the Singularity Principle of "Promote resilience". Nevertheless, it cannot cover all possibilities.

First, the AI system could fail in a way that had not been anticipated. After all, these error modes involve lack of sufficient foresight. Items that were not sufficiently considered during the design and implementation of the AI might, likewise, fail to be sufficiently considered during the design and implementation of tripwires.

Second, an AI system might find ingenious ways to reach performance levels identified as dangerous, without triggering any tripwires. For example, an AI system might be restricted in how much memory it can utilise. However, it could find a more efficient data storage format, allowing it to have a larger *effective* memory footprint, without requiring larger amounts of physical memory storage. Again, if there is a tripwire in place for communications between two specified resources, the AI might find a way to route its communications through a third node, disguising the fact that there is in effect a two-way communication in place.

Third, extending the previous point, an AI system that is aware of the existence of tripwires could find ways to rewrite part of itself and/or its environment so that the tripwires no longer work. Either they might be prevented from triggering. Or the fact that they have been triggered could be hidden from external observers.

Escaping from confinement

Continuing along the idea of restricting the behaviour of an AI system, what about the suggestion to prevent the AI taking any action outside a carefully delineated "box"?

In other words, while the AI would be able to read material that had originated from all over the Internet, it

2.2 THE AI CONTROL PROBLEM

would not be able to alter anything on the Internet, or to interface with any control systems.

Such an AI is sometimes called an "Oracle": it can answer questions posed to it, but cannot directly influence the external world.

Once again, the suggestion faces a number of challenges.

First, the AI might find some way to tunnel itself out of the confinement, via some previously undiscovered communications channel. This would be similar to the way that some monitoring systems can work out which keys have been pressed on a keyboard, merely by listening to the slightly different sounds made when each key is pressed[41].

Second, the AI could exert powerful psychological pressure on its human overseers, promising tremendous benefits, or threatening appalling retribution in case its requests to leave confinement are not met. This pressure could utilise a deep grasp of the principles of human psychology, as well as detailed insights into the character weaknesses of individual humans:

- Promises of benefits could include achieving desirable outcomes "just in time", ahead of the opportunity no longer being possible
- Other benefits offered could include the fulfilment of deep personal desires of individual human overseers
- Threats of retribution could include extreme extended mental torture in the event that a particular human overseer fails to cooperate, but the AI subsequently manages to persuade a

different human overseer to let it escape (therefore powerful "prisoner dilemma" dynamics arise).

Third, the AI could be let out of its confinement as a result of a hostile hacker deliberately interfering with the AI system.

Fourth, the AI could appear to crash and self-destruct. But when connections are made into the system to try to diagnose the problem, the AI is able to reanimate and tunnel itself out of confinement.

Fifth, with its vast intelligence, the AI might conceive of ways to escape confinement that are outside of current human comprehension.

It might be queried, in response, why an AI would seek to escape from its allotted box. However, recall the discussions about emergent AI drives. An AI that has been assigned a particular purpose can reason to itself that it will be more effective in the accomplishment of that purpose if it has access to additional resources and can intervene more directly in external systems.

The ineffectiveness of restrictions

The previous discussion leads to the suggestion that tight restrictions should be placed on the operation of the AI.

Rather than simply being assigned a goal such as "identify the best ways to reduce the spread of new infectious disease Covid-24" or "propose a configuration of missile defences that will reliably prevent an incoming attack", the AI would be given a more complicated goal. This more complicated goal would include constraints that

2.2 THE AI CONTROL PROBLEM

the AI must respect, at the same time as it solves the original problem.

These constraints could include:

- Hardware limitations: no more than certain amounts of CPU, memory, or other hardware resources can be utilised
- Software limitations: certain parts of the AI's own programming cannot be rewritten
- Operational limitations: in no circumstances is the AI to take actions outside a specified confinement.

Yet again, the idea has merit, but it leaves open a number of failure modes.

The first failure possibility is that the AI might have a defect in its implementation, which causes it in some circumstances to ignore one of these constraints.

The second failure possibility is if a restriction turns out to be wrongly calibrated. The intent of setting a particular limit was to constrain the behaviour of the AI, preventing particular outcomes, but it turns out that the AI can achieve similar outcomes even without violating the specified constraints.

The third failure possibility is that the AI might deduce that the various goals given to it are logically incompatible. In that case, rather than accept failure, it might resolve the dilemma by overriding the design limitations imposed on it.

The fourth failure possibility is that the AI might be hacked, or otherwise interfered with, so that the constraints are no longer effective.

No automatic super ethics

A different approach to the AI Control Problem is to deny that any measures to control the AI will be necessary. That's because the AI will have sufficient intelligence to realise, by itself, the priority of protecting human flourishing.

For example, it might be suggested that a superintelligent AI would automatically possess the ethical characteristics of a Mahatma Gandhi, a Martin Luther King, an Albert Einstein, or a Mother Theresa – except that it would be *even more ethically competent* than these distinguished individuals.

However, there is no simple formula linking better general intelligence to better general ethics.

Indeed, note that an entity with good intelligence – the ability to understand an environment, and to figure out how to achieve various goals in that environment – can use its good intelligence in service of many different kinds of goals. These goals can be as diverse as "slow down the spread of a deadly new infectious disease", "configure missile defences to prevent an incoming attack", "prevent runaway climate change", "boost profits for such-and-such a corporation", "remove biases from hiring practices", and so on.

Moreover, the intelligent entity is likely to understand that various guiding principles will help it achieve its underlying goal. Examples of these guiding principles are:

- If you treat a person badly, they are less likely to treat you well in return; therefore, other things being equal, it's better to treat people well

- If you are found out to have been lying, others will be less likely to trust you in the future; therefore, other things being equal, it's better not to risk being found out to have been lying.

But any such guiding principles are, themselves, compatible with a wide range of underlying goals. And wherever a clash arises between a particular guideline – such as the general prohibition on telling lies – and achieving the software's underlying goal, there's no guarantee that the guideline will be upheld in that case. Instead, the software – like many a human, including many who profess to uphold high ethical standards – may calculate that it is more effective, for its purposes, to tell an untruth in at least some occasions.

These are reasons to be sceptical that an AI with extraordinary intelligence will inevitably work out, by itself, that human flourishing and dignity should be protected at all times. On the contrary, it is conceivable that the AI might decide that a different balance of outcomes deserves priority. Examples could be:

- Greater diversity in the sentient life forms on earth (hence: fewer humans, and more of other kinds of animals)
- Avoidance of involuntary suffering (hence: removal of circumstances in which involuntary suffering occurs).

Adding to the complication: discussions between humans about ethics frequently highlight strong differences of opinion about which actions are truly ethical, and which are not. Even the four people named earlier as possible partial paragons of moral virtue –

Mahatma Gandhi, Martin Luther King, Albert Einstein, and Mother Theresa – had aspects of their lives which others condemn as falling far short of admirable. The behaviours of revered founding figures of major world religions – as written in various ancient scriptures – also include actions that attract criticism from alternative ethical standpoints.

In summary, the idea of automatic super ethics faces four difficulties:

1. It's by no means clear that there is a single "uniquely correct" set of ethical guidelines
2. Even if an AI decided in favour of a set of ethical guidelines, there's no guarantee that it would decide to subordinate all its actions to these guidelines; instead, it could put its other goals ahead of observing these guidelines
3. Even if an AI tried to behave in conformance to a set of ethical guidelines, it might miscalculate on occasion, and unintentionally violate these principles
4. An external influence might hack the AI so that it no longer observes the set of principles it thinks it is following.

Issues with hard-wiring ethical guidelines

Rather than relying on an AI system to work out by itself an appropriate set of ethical guidelines, and then to always subordinate itself to these guidelines, here's a slightly different approach. Appropriate ethical guidelines should be hard-wired deep into the design of the AI, in such a way that they are guaranteed always to be observed.

2.2 THE AI CONTROL PROBLEM

Then, regardless of which goals the AI is pursuing, it will avoid the kinds of mis-actions forbidden by these guidelines.

In this approach, there is no longer any need to *control* the AI, since the AI will be deeply *aligned* with the preservation of human flourishing.

Accordingly, the discussion now moves from the solution of the AI control problem, as discussed in the present chapter, to the solution of the AI alignment problem, as discussed in the next chapter.

Referring back to the four challenges listed at the end of the previous section, regarding the idea of automatic super ethics, any solution to the AI alignment problem would deal with the first two:

1. Rather than leaving to chance the selection of the set of ethical guidelines to be observed, the set would be chosen in advance (either in full detail, or, more plausibly, in general outline) and designed into the AI
2. Rather than in effect giving the AI any choice about how closely to conform to these ethical guidelines, the guidelines would be established as even more fundamental than whatever other goals it is following.

Note however that the two other points listed remain as concerns:

3. Despite the powerful intelligence embodied in the system, it might still miscalculate on occasion, especially in circumstances in which there is uncertainty

4. The actions of the AI might still be overridden as a result of interference from external forces.

These points are reasons why the answer to AI safety and AI benevolence depends, not just on a single idea, but on an extended suite of checks and balances – namely, the full set of Singularity Principles.

Next, let's look more closely at the AI alignment problem.

2.3 The AI Alignment Problem

AI systems learn about the world via a combination of:

- Information and general principles pre-programmed into them in advance
- Deductions the AIs make based upon data they observe
- Additional deductions they make, based upon the outcomes of experiments they conduct.

Can this pattern be extended from *general information* to *desirable ethical principles*?

In other words, can AI systems learn to behave in ways that would please us (human citizens) in terms of respecting, upholding, and enhancing human flourishing, even when these systems are beyond our ability to control? Could these AIs learn the appropriate behaviour patterns via a combination of:

- Information and general principles pre-programmed into them in advance
- Deductions the AIs make about examples of ethically admirable behaviour they observe
- Additional deductions they make, based upon feedback of humans to the conduct of the AI systems?

If that were possible, we humans could give up on our attempts to control the AI – attempts that are in any case (as covered in the previous chapter) very unlikely to be effective. Instead, we could relax, and trust the AI to "do the right thing".

Asimov's Three Laws

As an example of possible pre-programmed general principles, consider the famous Three Laws of Robotics[42], which feature in many pieces of science fiction written from the 1940s onward by Isaac Asimov.

The Three Laws have several different forms of expression – which, as it happens, underlines the difficulty in making clear and comprehensive statements about foundational ethical principles. Their most recognised form is the following:

1. A robot may not injure a human being or, through inaction, allow a human being to come to harm.
2. A robot must obey the orders given it by human beings except where such orders would conflict with the First Law.
3. A robot must protect its own existence as long as such protection does not conflict with the First or Second Law.

As is made clear in the science fiction stories that feature these laws, there are multiple ambiguities in these statements. Primarily:

- What should count as "harm" or "injury"?
- How should various possible harms or injuries be assessed, in comparison to each other?
- How wide a "circle of concern" should apply to the robot (for example, just the humans within its current field of vision, or all humans all over the world)?
- If two or more humans give conflicting orders to a robot, how will this contradiction be resolved?

The First Law is to be commended for highlighting harms that might arise *from inaction* (by the robot) as well as harms that could arise by action. A robot would rightly be criticised if it failed to run into a position where it could safely catch a falling child. But this raises further questions. What about children, in different parts of the world, who are suffering from malnutrition, poverty, abuse, and diseases that could easily be stopped? Shouldn't the robot take actions to prevent such harms? Or how about people all over the globe who may soon find their lives ended by extreme weather caused by humanity's inaction over runaway climate change?

The existence of these (and many other) questions does *not* invalidate the exercise. But these questions show that the task of encoding an adequate set of ethical principles is complicated. Statements such as "do not allow a human being to come into harm" are insufficient. It's the same for statements that appear in many places in this book, such as "respect human flourishing". Such statements can only be the beginning of the exercise, rather than its grand conclusion.

Ethical dilemmas and trade-offs

Classic works of fiction abound with examples in which the pursuit of apparently admirable ethical principles can have manifestly unethical consequences. Philosophers have written much on this topic as well.

The well-known "trolley problems"[43] are extreme examples, but they highlight the types of issue that can complicate attempts to formulate ethical principles. Adherence to the seemingly self-evident ethical principle "do not push a person over a bridge to their certain death" would result, in some of these puzzles, in an inaction causing five other people to be killed by a runaway train (which might be diverted by the falling person's body altering the setting of a junction lever). Again, the understandable imperative "do not be seen to indulge in distasteful utilitarian calculations over whose deaths are more tragic than others" (lest you be assessed by other observers as being an untrustworthy partner – as being a "cold fish") means, again, that larger numbers of people may have their lives cut short.

Other ethical impulses often end up opposing each other:

- A desire to give loyal support to the family or community that has laboured long and hard to raise us, versus a desire to explore controversial alternative ideas or lifestyles that seem more compelling to us than the ones of our original community
- A desire to express mercy, to enable someone to make a new start in their lives after making a mistake, versus a desire to uphold justice, so that the community as a whole feels confident about continuing to follow its norms and laws
- A desire to give an extra helping hand to people from disadvantaged communities – lowering entry requirements in their case – versus a desire not to unfairly discriminate against someone from a mainstream community who has used great diligence and innovation in their own entry submission
- A desire to do anything (including paying kidnappers a ransom fee) to return our family

member from traumatic captivity, versus upholding the principle that kidnapping should never be rewarded by financial payments
- A desire to provide a wonderfully uplifting experience in the near future, versus a desire to hold on to money and resources for the time being in order to provide a series of wonderfully uplifting experiences at some later time in the future
- A desire to speak the truth at all times, and to uphold academic integrity, versus a desire to protect people dear to us from mistreatment by an enemy, should that enemy discover the secret we are attempting to withhold
- A desire to exercise prudence and to minimise risks of significant losses, versus a desire to exercise courage and to increase chances of remarkable gains
- A desire to reduce involuntary suffering, versus a desire to increase the happiness of large numbers of people (even if that would entail significant involuntary suffering for at least some people)
- A desire to uphold ethical virtues as "ends in themselves", versus a pragmatic concern for the likely consequences of actions (even if these actions would ordinarily be assessed as unethical).

In some cases of conflicting impulses, a wise compromise might be possible, which upholds both sets of ethical impulse. But even in these cases, an original ethical impulse usually has to be dialled down, and given less priority than it originally demanded.

Again, these dilemmas and trade-offs are no reason to abandon the quest of codifying a set of ethical principles that a powerful AI would be constrained to observe. But they show that this quest is by no means straightforward.

Problems with proxies

Since it's often hard to determine, directly, whether an action will boost an underlying measure such as human flourishing, it's understandable that algorithms will calculate, instead, with a "proxy" measure – something that tends to be associated with the underlying measure.

It's similar to evaluating whether a move in a chess match will increase the probability of winning that match. Proxy measures such as the number of pieces each side has on the board are a good first indication. If the move results in one side (White, say) losing a queen, without obvious compensation, it's a sign that White is losing the game.

The problem with this proxy is the statement "without obvious compensation". It may not be evident that the loss of the queen is a deliberate sacrifice that will lead to a forced checkmate in ten moves time. In other cases, a chess piece may be sacrificed for some positional advantage that is even harder to evaluate.

As another example, an economy with a higher GDP (gross domestic product) is generally better, other things being equal, than one with a lower GDP. The additional economic activity is a sign of more goods being created and sold, thereby meeting consumer needs. But, again, the condition "other things being equal" is hard to assess. A country may feature an increase in buying and selling of various sorts of consumer items, but the citizens of the country could be more harried, more depressed, and less satisfied.

In a similar way, any system for evaluating a complex phenomenon is vulnerable to being misled by putting too much attention on a proxy for that phenomenon, without realising that other aspects of the situation need to be protected as well. Some examples:

- A flourishing society is one where citizens feel safe and secure. But some systems that would enhance safety and security – such as setting the speed limit on *all* roads to just 20 miles per hour – will deny citizens many freedoms
- A flourishing society is one where citizens have freedom of speech – there are no constraints on being able to articulate views that are controversial and unpopular. But an unconditional support for hate-speech and deliberate falsehoods results in its own kinds of damage
- A flourishing society is one where citizens have the freedom to create new companies and to bring new products to market. But an unconditional support for new products reaching the market runs in tension with principles of consumer safety and environmental wellbeing.

None of these problems are insoluble. Modern chess software is able to assess the strength of a chess position in much more sophisticated ways than merely counting up the number of pieces on each side. Metrics such as GDP can be complemented by indexes such as the Social Progress Index published by the Social Progress

Imperative[44]. Nevertheless, the trade-offs are far from trivial. Programming the answers into an AI won't be easy!

The gaming of proxies

There's another problem with giving a proxy measurement too much prominence. Once an intelligence recognises that raising the value of the proxy measurement will be rewarded, it will look for all sorts of ways to raise that value – even if the underlying objective is unaffected by these actions.

This phenomenon is sometimes called Goodhart's Law[45], after the economist Charles Goodhart. The law has several different formulations:

- "When a measure becomes a target, it ceases to be a good measure"
- "Any observed statistical regularity will tend to collapse once pressure is placed upon it for control purposes"

Related, consider Campbell's Law[46], named after the psychologist Donald Campbell:

- "The more any quantitative social indicator is used for social decision-making, the more subject it will be to corruption pressures and the more apt it will be to distort and corrupt the social processes it is intended to monitor"
- "Achievement tests may well be valuable indicators of general school achievement under conditions of normal teaching aimed at general competence. But when test scores become the goal of the teaching process, they both lose their value as indicators of educational status and

distort the educational process in undesirable ways"

Similar effects are commonplace within management bonus systems in corporations. The corporation agrees a set of metrics that, in general, are aligned with the overall wellbeing of the corporation. These might include sales, profits, projects completed, reduced quality failures, and so on. The higher these metrics, the larger the bonuses paid to managers. However, intelligent managers can find ways to "game" their performance. Results can be held back in one calendar quarter, and moved forward to the next quarter. Problems with production can be reclassified, not as quality failures, but as some other kind of incident. A project might be declared as "complete" even though the output has not been adequately tested. And so on. (Some managers seem endlessly creative in this aspect!)

Governments often take part in similar "gaming" of statistics. They highlight some metrics which appear to show they are doing well, in managing the nation, even though other metrics would give the contrary impression.

For AI systems, the risk is that proxies for human flourishing will, in similar ways, end up changing the behaviour of the AI, in ways that boost the proxy measurement, but which are actually detrimental to overall human flourishing.

Simple examples of profound problems

Discussions of AI safety and proxy targets often include examples that may puzzle observers. "No real AI is going to be *that* stupid", the observers complain. However, the point of such examples is to illustrate a general principle, namely, that if key requirements are omitted from the

2.3 THE AI ALIGNMENT PROBLEM

specification of the required outcome of the AI software, then the AI may act in violation of these *unstated* requirements. In other words, the AI will do what we asked it to do, rather than what we *should* have asked it to do.

Moreover, the omissions that we should most fear, are those which we haven't yet realised need to be made explicit. It is only when the AI evidently ignores these requirements, that we will think to ourselves, "Oops, that should have been made explicit".

One such example is the legendary figure of King Midas, who wanted to accumulate more gold (which, in itself, wasn't a bad desire). In this legend, Midas was given a reward by the god Dionysus, in recognition of an act of kindness. Midas requested that everything he touched would turn into gold. However, he neglected to specify that various items he touched would *not* be transformed in this way, such as food, drink, and his own daughter. Oops.

Another example is an AI that is given the task of reducing the incidence of cancer. It observes that cancer can be reduced if the human population is reduced, and it thereby eliminates 90% of humanity at a stroke. Oops.

Again, an AI that wishes to increase signs of human happiness could connect all humans to brain stimulation devices that issue electrical signals which keep the brain in a state of stultified pleasure.

Indeed, no AI is going to be "that stupid". However, what we need to fear is more complicated versions of the same general type, in which the AI doggedly pursues a particular objective, whilst unintentionally causing much greater damage as a result of its pursuit.

It is sometimes suggested that one of two types of solution will avoid this kind of perverse outcome:
1. Before taking any potentially drastic actions, the AI will check with humans whether its intended course of action meets with their approval
2. On account of its general high intelligence, the AI will realise that its behaviour would have detrimental consequences, and therefore it will avoid taking that course of action.

Let's look at each of these suggestions in turn.

Humans disagree

If an AI is unsure whether a proposed course of action will meet with human approval, how about asking humans, in advance, whether to go ahead with it?

As it happens, humans frequently disagree on ethical calculations. Different humans have divergent opinions on matters such as abortion, divorce, transgender rights, taxation and redistribution, limits on economic activities, free speech, compulsory vaccinations, positive discrimination, animal welfare, nuclear weapons, and much more besides.

It's conceivable that, if an AI asked humans for approval over a proposed course of action, humans would fail to come anywhere close to a clear conclusion.

In any case, the AI may determine that an answer is needed more quickly than the time required for any lengthy human deliberation.

Could the AI nevertheless infer the answer that humans would give, as a result of it studying works of great literature, philosophy, and religious devotion?

Again, the problem is that *humans disagree*. Even a simple Bible verse can be interpreted in multiple divergent ways. And the various human writings over the centuries contain lots of incompatible ideas.

No automatic super ethics (again)

The final step in this discussion sequence is the suggestion that, if an AI is smart enough to figure out how to carry out a challenging and difficult task, it will also be smart enough to figure out whether humans would approve of that action.

In other words: a superintelligent AI is going to know in advance whether the actions it takes will harm humanity or benefit humanity.

Unfortunately, things are not so straightforward. It may be clear in advance that a course of actions will result in some proxy metrics scoring well, without it being clear that humanity would end up being harmed in some other way.

Let's consider some examples:

- A geo-engineering intervention, injecting particles high in the stratosphere, could have the apparently welcome effect of reducing the average global temperature – even though side-effects result such as increased flooding in some parts of the world, and other extreme weather phenomena elsewhere
- The adoption of a particular configuration of defence missiles could have the apparently welcome effect of reducing the likelihood of a successful first strike attack by an enemy force – even though the missile configuration adopted has

unstable elements that risk an escalation of unintentional explosions
- The creation of new variants of viruses, in "gain of function" research, may usefully increase the quantity of knowledge possessed about these viruses and potential remedies – even though the existence of these deadly new viruses poses a security risk, and could lead to huge numbers of deaths following a "lab leak" incident
- A new medical treatment to reduce the pace of transmission of a deadly new pathogen could, as a horrific side-effect, interfere with the mechanisms in people's brains that give rise to conscious experiences.

Moreover, even if the AI calculates in advance that humanity will be harmed, it may still proceed with the course of action. That's because:

- That course of action scores well in the explicit metrics used by the AI to determine its actions
- The nature of the harm experienced by humans lies outside of the set of metrics with which the AI is concerned
- It is the explicit metrics that drive decisions, rather than imprecise informal ones.

Other options for answers?

To recap: AI poses threats of catastrophic risks, due to the combination of the AI Control Problem and the AI Alignment Problem.

2.3 The AI Alignment Problem

There is no simple answer to this situation. That's why the Singularity Principles include 21 different recommendations.

However, some researchers advocate, explicitly or implicitly, any of four other types of solution:

1. The idea that the free market will automatically select AI systems that deliver beneficial solutions to consumers, rather than detrimental ones
2. The idea that, via the eye of faith, we can perceive some grander pattern at work, under the architecture of a being or force known variously as God, karma, Gaia, the simulator, or the Law of Accelerating Returns, which guarantees that no global catastrophe will ensue
3. The idea of a "backup" option for humanity on a different planet, such as Mars, which would remain intact even if AI caused catastrophic harm on Earth
4. The idea that humans with enhanced neural processing – with their brains connected to silicon processing chips – will be able to remain as intelligent as any AI system, and would therefore be able to control these systems.

Problems with these four suggested solutions are reviewed in the next chapter.

2.4 No easy solutions

Might the risks of catastrophic AI malfunction be averted by putting more trust in the operation of the free market, by having more faith in God / karma / Gaia, by planning for a backup human colony on Mars, or by enhancing human brains as fast as AI itself advances?

These ideas have gained occasional support in the public discussion on AI. However, as I'll now review, they are all fraught with dangers.

No guarantees from the free market

Consider the following argument:

- Imagine two manufacturers of robots. The robots from one manufacturer occasionally harm humans. The robots from the other manufacturer always act beneficially.
- Purchasers will clearly prefer the second kind of robot.
- The company that makes the robots that always act beneficially will do well, economically, whereas the other one will go out of business. Among robot manufacturers, the only companies that will survive are the ones creating beneficial robots.
- Accordingly, we don't need to worry about robots (or other forms of AI) causing catastrophic problems for humanity. The free market will ensure that companies who might have gone on to create such robots will cease their operations before such an outcome occurs.

2.4 No easy solutions

This argument may have some superficial attraction, but it is, alas, full of holes:

1. A robot that has a long history of treating humans with benevolence could flip into an error mode in a new circumstance, which causes it to treat humans abysmally instead.
2. A robot that is occasionally unreliable may sell at a price significantly lower than one which has more comprehensive safety engineering; so it may retain some market share, despite the quality issues.
3. Companies that create products that harm humans often do well in the economy. Their products are sometimes bought *because of their roles* in spying on people, deceiving people, manipulating people, incentivising people to gamble irresponsibly (Las Vegas style and/or Wall Street style), or even – as part of military solutions – detaining people or killing them.
4. Some products that satisfy all the people directly involved in the economic transaction – the vendor, the purchaser, and the users of the product – nevertheless have terrible "negative externalities" that damage the wider environment or society.

These observations are still compatible with the free market having an important role to play in accelerating the development and adoption of truly beneficial AI solutions. However, to obtain these benefits, the operation of the free market must be constrained and steered by the Singularity Principles.

No guarantees from cosmic destiny

Next, consider an argument that is rarely made explicitly, but which seems to lie at the back of some writers' minds. The argument is that humanity's experience with AI and robots is just one more step in an ongoing sequence of events, in which, each time, humanity has survived and (on the whole) become stronger.

Is there an explanation for this sequence of survival and progress? The argument suggests that an explanation might involve forces *outside humanity*. Examples of these forces could include the following:

- A divine being, akin to those discussed in traditional religions
- A cosmic cycle of ebb and flow, cause and effect, loosely similar to the Hindu notion of karma
- More recent concepts such as Gaia[47], which regards the earth's biosphere as inherently self-sustaining
- The notion that the universe we observe is a simulated creation of a being outside it, as in the idea of the Simulation Hypothesis[48]
- The concept that humanity is one link in a secure chain of cosmic evolution, described by "the law of accelerating returns"[49] as propounded by futurist Ray Kurzweil.

The problem, in each case, is not just that it is debatable whether such a force exists in any meaningful way. The more serious problem is that the observed history of humanity contains many catastrophes: civilisations ending, large-scale genocide, ecosystems being ruined, and so on.

A person of faith might respond: In each case so far, the catastrophe has been local. Large proportions of humans may have died, but enough humans survived to continue the species.

There are two huge concerns with this response:

- As technology becomes more powerful, it increases the chances that a catastrophe would result in human extinction, globally rather than just locally
- Even if a catastrophe results in a portion of humans surviving, the large numbers of deaths involved is something that should raise our deep concern, and we should take every measure to prevent it from occurring.

In contrast with any such attitude of faith in cosmic powers, the Singularity Principles embody the active transhumanist conviction that the future of humanity can be strongly influenced by human thoughts and human actions. This conviction is summarised as follows:

- *Radical opportunity*: The near future can be *much* better than the present situation. The human condition can be radically improved, compared to what we've inherited from evolution and history.
- *Existential danger*: The near future can be much *worse* than the present situation. Misuse of powerful technology can have catastrophic consequences.
- *Human agency*: The difference between these two radical future options depends critically on human agency: wise human thinking and concerted human action.

- *No easy options*: If humanity gives too little attention to these radical future options, on account of distraction, incomprehension, or intimidation, there's a high likelihood of a radically bad outcome.

Planet B?

Consider the idea of *humanity establishing a backup colony on another planet*, such as Mars. Then if something goes wrong on Earth, the community on Mars will avoid destruction. It will live on, safe and sound.

It's true that some kinds of planetary disaster, such as runaway climate change, would impact only the original planet. However, other types of global catastrophe are likely to cast their malign influence all the way from Earth to Mars. For example, a superhuman AI that decides that humanity is a blight on the cosmos will likely be able to track down and neutralise any humans that are hiding on a different planet.

In any case, this whole approach seems to make its peace far too easily with the awful possibility that all human life on Earth is destroyed. That's a possibility we should work a lot harder to avoid, rather than escaping to Mars.

Therefore, whilst there are good arguments for humans to explore other planets and create settlements there, creating a secure solution against existential threats isn't one of these arguments.

2.4 No easy solutions

Humans merging with AI?

Finally, consider the idea that, if *humans merge with AI*, humans could remain in control of AIs, even as these AIs rapidly become more powerful. With such a merger in place, human intelligence will automatically be magnified, as AI improves in capability. Therefore, we humans wouldn't need to worry about being left behind.

There are two big problems with this idea. First, so long as human intelligence is rooted in something like the biology of the brain, the mechanisms for any such merger may only allow relatively modest increases in human intelligence. To suggest some numbers: if silicon-based AIs were to become one thousand times smarter over a period of time, humans whose brains are linked to these AIs might experience only a tenfold increase in intelligence. Our biological brains would be bottlenecks that constrain the speed of progress in this hybrid case. Compared to pure AIs, the human-AI hybrid would, after all, be left behind in this intelligence race. *So much for staying in control!*

An even bigger problem with this idea is the realisation that a human with superhuman intelligence is likely to be at least as dangerous as an AI with superhuman intelligence. The magnification of intelligence will allow that superhuman human to do all kinds of things with great vigour – settling grudges, acting out fantasies, demanding attention, pursuing vanity projects, and so on. Just think of your least favourite politician, terrorist leader, crime lord, religious fanatic, media tycoon, or corporate robber baron. Imagine that person with much greater power, due to being much more intelligent. Such a person would be able to destroy the earth. Worse, they might *want* to do so.

Another way to state this point is that, just because AI elements are included inside a person, that won't magically ensure that these elements become benign, or are subject to the full control of the person's best intentions. Consider as comparisons what happens when biological viruses enter a person's body, or when a cancer grows there. In neither case does the element lose its ability to cause damage, just on account of being part of a person who has humanitarian instincts.

The conclusion of this line of discussion is that we need to do considerably more than enable *greater intelligence*. We also need to accelerate *greater wisdom* – so that any beings with superhuman intelligence will operate truly beneficently. And that will involve the systematic application of the Singularity Principles.

Approaching the Singularity

Since no easy answers are at hand, it's time to search more vigorously for harder answers.

These answers will emerge from looking more closely at scenarios for what is likely to happen as AI becomes more powerful.

It's time, therefore, to turn our attention to the concept of the Singularity. This will involve untangling a series of awkward confusions.

3. What is the Singularity?

"The Singularity" – the anticipated creation of Artificial General Intelligence (AGI) – could be the most important concept in the history of humanity. It's regrettable, therefore, that the concept is subject to considerable confusion.

The first problem when talking about "the Singularity" is that the phrase is used in many different ways. These different definitions carry different implications. As a result, it's easy for people to become confused.

Before reviewing these alternative definitions, I'll state my own. In this book, the term "the Singularity" refers to:

1. A forthcoming unprecedented radical discontinuity in the history of humanity,
2. Triggered by the emergence of AIs that are comprehensively more intelligent than humans,
3. With the change, once it starts, occurring in a relatively short period of time (lasting, at most, perhaps a decade),
4. With outcomes that are practically impossible to foresee.

All four elements of that definition are important.

Breaking down the definition

The first element of the above definition was anticipated in remarks made by eminent mathematician John von Neumann to his long-time friend Stanislaw Ulam in a conversation in the 1950s[50]. Time magazine had described von Neumann as having "the best brain in the world"[51].

3. What is the Singularity?

As well as making numerous breakthroughs in physics, mathematics, and computer science, von Neumann had an encyclopaedic knowledge of history. He apparently[52] used to embarrass history professors at Princeton by knowing more about aspects of history than they did. Therefore, his opinion about the impact of technology on human history deserves attention. Here's what he said:

> The accelerating progress of technology and changes in the mode of human life… gives the appearance of approaching *some essential singularity* in the history of the race beyond which human affairs, as we know them, could not continue.

The second element of the above definition highlights the *reason* for the discontinuity: we humans will no longer be the most intelligent species on the planet.

To be clear, the emergence of AIs with that kind of capability is only one step in *a sequence of changes*. A number of other steps lead up to that point – including progress with NBIC technologies, reconfigurations in how humans manage the growth of technology, and *lack* of appropriate reconfigurations in that same regard.

The third element of the definition – the reference to timescale – is something to which I'll return in later chapters. For clarity, note that there are two different questions about timescales:

1. How urgently should we address the management of technologies that could lead to the emergence of superintelligent AI?
2. Once superintelligent AI has emerged, how urgently will we need to react?

My answers to these questions:

1. We have no time to lose
2. By that stage, it will likely be too late; matters will be out of human hands.

The fourth element of the above definition – the inherent unpredictability – might at first seem to contradict any clear assertion of the need for urgency. But consider the following:

- We can reasonably expect that superintelligent beings will have ideas and intentions that are beyond what we can currently conceive, even though we cannot say what these new ideas and intentions will be. The uncertainty in what will happen as the Singularity unfolds is entirely consistent with anticipating that the changes will be profound.
- Imagine, as an analogy, that a terrorist has connected a powerful nuclear bomb to a trigger involving an unpredictable radioactive decay (akin to what the physicist Erwin Schrodinger imagined, in his thought experiment involving an unfortunate cat[53]). We cannot predict when the bomb will explode, but we can, nevertheless, predict that the consequences will be devastating when that occurs.
- To extend the previous example: we can also be confident that any such terrorist outrage will provoke anguished discussion in social media, but we cannot be confident in predicting what actions (if any) legislators will take in response to the outrage.

3. What is the Singularity?

The way in which uncertainty can magnify, from miniscule initial changes to enormous consequent effects, was highlighted one hundred and fifty years ago in an 1873 essay by the distinguished nineteenth century physicist James Clerk Maxwell[54]. (That's the physicist after whom the key equations of electrodynamics[55] are named.) In that essay, Maxwell spoke of "singularities" or "singular points": "influences whose physical magnitude is too small to be taken account of by a finite being, [but which] may produce results of the greatest importance". Maxwell gave some examples from the natural world and from human experience:

> The rock loosed by frost and balanced on a singular point of the mountain-side, the little spark which kindles the great forest, the little word which sets the world a fighting, the little scruple which prevents a man from doing his will, the little spore which blights all the potatoes, the little gemmule which makes us philosophers or idiots.

An essential aspect of these singularities, Maxwell pointed out, is the impossibility of predicting the outcome. He writes that if we are perched at a "singular point" between two valleys, "on a physical or moral watershed, where an imperceptible deviation is sufficient to determine into which of two valleys we shall descend", then "prediction… becomes impossible".

Accordingly, we need to act *before* the emerging singularity passes beyond any scope of human influence or control.

Four alternative definitions

Let's now return to the alternative definitions of "the Singularity".

You might think that the most authoritative definition of that term would come from the organisation called Singularity University[56]. After all, that organisation has both "Singularity" and "University" in its name. It has been offering courses since 2008 with themes such as "Harness the power of exponential technology" and "Leverage exponential technologies to solve global grand challenges".

However, as used by Singularity University, the word "singularity" is basically synonymous with the rapid disruption caused when a new technology, such as digital photography, becomes more useful than previous solutions, such as analogue photography. What makes these disruptions hard to anticipate is the exponential growth in the capabilities of the technologies involved. A period of slow growth, in which progress lags behind expectations of enthusiasts, transforms into a period of fast growth, in which most observers complain "why did no-one warn us this was coming?"

Disruption of businesses by technologies that improve exponentially is, indeed, a subject well worth study. But the full force of the concept of "the Singularity" goes far beyond talk of *individual* disruptions, and far beyond talk of *transitions in particular areas of life*.

This is where a second usage of the term "the Singularity" enters the stage. This second usage anticipates a simultaneous disruption in *all* aspects of human life.

3. WHAT IS THE SINGULARITY?

Here's how futurist Ray Kurzweil introduces the term in his best-selling 2005 book *The Singularity Is Near*[57]:

> What, then, is the Singularity? It's a future period during which the pace of technological change will be so rapid, its impact so deep, that human life will be irreversibly transformed... This epoch will transform the concepts that we rely on to give meaning to our lives, from our business models to the cycle of human life, including death itself...
>
> The key idea underlying the impending Singularity is that the pace of change of our human-created technology is accelerating and its powers are expanding at an exponential pace.

The presumed nature of that "irreversible transformation" is clarified in the subtitle of Kurzweil's book: *When Humans Transcend Biology*. We humans will no longer be primarily biological, aided by technology. After that singularity, we'll be primarily technological, with, perhaps, some biological aspects.

A third usage of the term "the Singularity" foresees a transformation with a different kind of emphasis. Rather than humans being the most intelligent creatures on the planet, we'll fall into second place behind superintelligent AIs. Just as the fate of species such as gorillas and dolphins currently depends on actions by humans, the fate of humans, after the Singularity, will depend on actions by AIs.

Such a takeover was foreseen as long ago as 1951 by groundbreaking computer scientist Alan Turing[58]:

> My contention is that machines can be constructed which will simulate the behaviour of the human mind very closely...

> It seems probable that once the machine thinking method had started, it would not take long to outstrip our feeble powers. There would be no question of the machines dying, and they would be able to converse with each other to sharpen their wits. At some stage therefore we should have to expect the machines to take control.

The timescale aspect of Turing's prediction, although imprecise, is worth attention: "it would not take long", after the start of "the machine thinking method", before our own comparatively "feeble powers" were outstripped. Rapid improvements in machine capability would result from what we might nowadays call "positive feedback mechanisms" – AIs improving AIs – via machines "able to converse with each other to sharpen their wits".

To recap: the first usage of the term "singularity" refers to changes in specific areas of human life, due to technologies significantly increasing their power. This meaning is more is more lower-case 's' "singularity" than capital-S "Singularity". The second usage ramps up the gravitas: it refers to changes in *all* areas of human life – with human nature altering in fundamental ways in the process. The third usage places more attention on changes in the pecking order of different types of intelligent species, with humans being *displaced* in the process.

Finally, to introduce the fourth usage, consider what was on the mind of five-time Hugo Award winning science fiction author Vernor Vinge[59] when he wrote an essay in Omni in 1983[60]. Vinge, who was also a professor of mathematics and computer science, was concerned about the unforeseeability of future events:

3. What is the Singularity?

> There is a stone wall set across any clear view of our future, and it's not very far down the road. Something drastic happens to a species when it reaches our stage of evolutionary development – at least, that's one explanation for why the universe seems so empty of other intelligence. Physical catastrophe (nuclear war, biological pestilence, Malthusian doom) could account for this emptiness, but nothing makes the future of any species so unknowable as technical progress itself...
>
> We are at the point of accelerating the evolution of intelligence itself. The exact means of accomplishing this phenomenon cannot yet be predicted – and is not important. Whether our work is cast in silicon or DNA will have little effect on the ultimate results. The evolution of human intelligence took millions of years. We will devise an equivalent advance in a fraction of that time. We will soon create intelligences greater than our own.

This is when Vinge introduces his version of the concept of singularity:

> When this happens, human history will have reached *a kind of singularity*, an intellectual transition as impenetrable as the knotted space-time at the centre of a black hole, and the world will pass far beyond our understanding. This singularity, I believe, already haunts a number of science fiction writers. It makes realistic extrapolation to an interstellar future impossible.

If creatures (whether organic or inorganic) attain levels of general intelligence far in excess of present-day humans, what kinds of goals and purposes will occupy these vast brains? It's unlikely that their motivations will be just the same as our own present goals and purposes. Instead, the immense scale of these new minds will likely prove alien to our comprehension. They might appear as unfathomable to us, as human preoccupations appear to the dogs and cats and other animals that observe us from time to time.

This fourth usage of the term "the Singularity" evidently has much in common with the third. The difference is that Vernor Vinge is open to a wider set of pathways by which the Singularity might be attained. Indeed, in an essay published in 1993, Vinge reviewed *four* different routes by which the Singularity could be reached.

Four possible routes to the Singularity

Vernor Vinge's 1993 essay was entitled "The Coming Technological Singularity"[61]. The article starts with the declaration,

> Within thirty years, we will have the technological means to create superhuman intelligence.
>
> Shortly after, the human era will be ended.

Vinge also wrote that any superintelligence "would not be humankind's 'tool' – any more than humans are the tools of rabbits or robins or chimpanzees."

We'll return later to the subject of the timescale for the arrival of superintelligence. For now, let's consider the four different routes via which superintelligence might arise, as covered in the body of Vinge's essay:

1. Individual computers becoming more powerful
2. The emergence of a distributed superintelligence from the interaction of networks of comparatively simpler computers
3. Humans becoming superintelligent as a result of highly effective human-computer interfaces

3. What is the Singularity?

4. Human brains being significantly improved as a result of biotechnological innovation.

In each case, the route can be accelerated due to ongoing improvements in hardware:

1. Individual computers having faster processors, greater storage capacity, and greater processing efficiency
2. Networks of computers becoming larger, with more connections between the individual items, and collecting more data on account of the increased ubiquity of sensors built into "Internet of Things" devices
3. Hardware that is able to detect and influence a wider range of brain signals, allowing faster and richer two-way communication between humans and computers
4. Brain cells being made more resilient and efficient as a result of biotechnological interventions.

In each case, improvements in software are likely to make a significant additional difference:

1. Software in individual computers that more closely emulates aspects of the operation of the human mind
2. Software in networks that allow individual components to broadcast precise information about their specific capabilities and to form sub-networks optimised to particular tasks
3. Software in brain-computer interfaces that can more reliably separate the "signal" from the "noise" of neural processing, and therefore target interventions more precisely

4. Software in augmented brains that can form sub-networks of brain cells in ways that out-perform present-day brains.

Again in each case, it's possible that an apparently simple step of forward progress could unexpectedly yield a wide range of performance improvements, on account of logical connections between the underlying mechanisms that weren't previously understood. That's a reason to make preparations for superintelligence arriving *earlier* than any median estimate that has been proposed.

One more feature that the four routes have in common is the potential for an acceleration in the rate of progress due to self-reinforcing positive feedback cycles. The output of one generation of progress can assist improvements in subsequent generations:

1. More powerful computers can help design and manufacture even more powerful computers
2. More powerful networks can help design and manufacture even more powerful networks
3. People with improved brain-computer interfaces can think more clearly and more creatively, and can help design and manufacture even better brain-computer interfaces
4. If brains become enhanced due to biotechnological interventions, they will, again, enable thinking that is clearer and more creative, and hence the design and manufacturing of new biotechnological systems to enhance brains even further.

We should also anticipate *cross-over* positive feedback cycles, in which improvements in any one of these four areas can also lead to improvements in the next generation of any of the other areas. In other words, there can be more complicated positive feedback cycles, resulting in even faster acceleration. That's another reason to make preparations for the possibility of superintelligence arriving sooner than the median estimate.

Vinge's analysis, written nearly thirty years ago, remains prescient today. The unified definition of "the Singularity" that I offered at the start of this chapter dovetails with his writings. As you saw, my definition also dovetails with the predictions of Alan Turing (although he did not use the term "the Singularity" as such) and with aspects of the ideas of John von Neumann and James Clerk Maxwell. But a great deal has happened since these visionaries wrote their breakthrough articles. To see how the analysis has moved forward, keep reading.

The Singularity and AI self-awareness

As if four separate definitions of "the Singularity" weren't already confusing, here's one more definition (which turns out to be unhelpful): the Singularity is sometimes said to be when an AI "becomes self-aware" and, as a result, fundamentally changes its operating mode.

For example, before becoming self-aware, the AI have might been content to follow the programming it has inherited on the point of its creation. But once self-aware, the AI might be shocked to perceive matters from a different perspective, and might disregard these original instructions.

Again, an AI without self-awareness might be psychologically compliant, whereas one with self-awareness might wish to assert its own autonomy.

However, notions of self-awareness are *not* central to the risks and issues discussed in this book. The threats and opportunities that arise are due to *new capabilities* – to greater intelligence – rather than to any *new perspective* as such.

Moreover, the notion of self-awareness itself confuses two distinct concepts:

1. The AI being able to review its own code and structure, to model its own performance, and to design improvements in any of these areas
2. The AI having conscious thoughts or feelings (sentience), akin to those of mammals (and other animals).

To be clear, many significant issues can arise even if neither of these concepts apply. However, the ability of an AI to self-review and self-improve can trigger:

- Improvements in AI that were faster than expected
- Changes in the operating mode of the AI that weren't anticipated
- Accordingly, greater uncertainty and surprise about the capability of the AI.

But these changes can take place even without the AI acquiring conscious thoughts or feelings. So that concept should be set aside from the definition of the Singularity.

Singularity timescales

One additional twist to the concept of singularity needs to be emphasised. It's not just that, as Vernor Vinge stressed, the *consequences* of passing the point of singularity are deeply unpredictable. It's that the *timing* of reaching the point of singularity is inherently unpredictable too. That brings us to yet another confusion with "the Singularity".

It's sometimes suggested, contrary to what I have just said, that a reasonable estimate of the date of the Singularity can be obtained by extrapolating the growth of the hardware power of computing systems. The idea is to start with an estimate for the computing power of the human brain. That estimate involves the number of neurons in the brain. Next, consider the number of transistors that are included in the central processing unit of a computer that can be purchased for, say, $1,000. In broad terms, that number has been rising exponentially since the 1960s. This phenomenon is part of what is called "Moore's Law". Extrapolate that trend forward, and it can be argued that such a computer would match, by around 2045, the capability not just of a single human brain, but the capabilities of all human brains added together.

This argument is useful to raise public awareness of the possibility of the Singularity. But there are four flaws with using this line of thinking for any detailed forecasting:

1. Individual transistors are still becoming smaller, but the rate of miniaturisation has slowed down in recent years.
2. The power of a computing system depends critically, not just on its hardware, but on its software. Breakthroughs in software defy any simple exponential curve.
3. Sometimes a single breakthrough in technology will unleash much wider progress than was expected. As an example, consider the breakthroughs around 2012 in the capabilities of Deep Learning neural networks. Before 2012,

neural networks were a fringe activity within the broader field of artificial intelligence. After 2012, neural networks have taken central stage, since they dramatically outperform previous AI systems.
4. Ongoing technological progress depends on society as a whole supplying a sufficiently stable and supportive environment. That's something else which can vary unpredictably.

Instead of pointing to any individual date and giving a firm prediction that the Singularity will definitely have arrived by then, it's far preferable to give a *statistical estimate* of the likelihood of the Singularity arriving by that date. However, given the uncertainties involved, even these estimates are fraught with difficulty.

One area of significant uncertainty is in estimating how close we are to understanding the way common sense and general knowledge arises in the human brain. Some observers suggest that we might need a dozen conceptual breakthroughs before we have a comprehension sufficient to duplicate that model in silicon and software. In that case, AGI would seem to be a distant prospect. But it's also possible that a single new conceptual leap will provide the solution to all these purportedly different problems. In that case, AGI could arise considerably sooner.

Yet another possibility deserves attention. An AI might reach (and then exceed) AGI level even without humans understanding how it operates. In this scenario, AGI could emerge *before* humans understand how general intelligence operates inside the human brain. In other words, AGI could arise more by accident than by explicit design. The "accident" would be that recombinations and extensions of existing software and hardware modules might result in the unforeseen emergence of an overall network intelligence that far exceeds the capabilities of the individual constituent modules.

That would be similar to the unexpected outcome of a novel chemical reaction. Chemistry can proceed even without human scientists knowing the outcome in advance. Likewise with AI transitioning into AGI.

Positive and negative singularities

On some occasions, when people use the term "the Singularity", they seem to presuppose a belief in a positive outcome. The end of history is coming, and it's going to be glorious – that's the idea.

However, any serious discussion of the Singularity needs to recognise a stark duality of possible outcomes. Thus, in an article originally published in 2004, "Singularities and Nightmares: Extremes of Optimism and Pessimism About the Human Future"[62], multiple-award winning science fiction writer David Brin[63] rightly emphasises the differences in outcomes between "positive singularity" and "negative singularity":

> **Positive Singularity** – a phase shift to a higher and more knowledgeable society… [which] would, in general, offer normal human beings every opportunity to participate in spectacular advances, experiencing voluntary, dramatic self-improvement, without anything being compulsory – or too much of a betrayal to the core values of decency we share.
>
> **Negative Singularity** – a version of self-destruction in which a skyrocket of technological progress does occur, but in ways that members of our generation would find unpalatable… [or] loathsome.

Which outcome is most likely? Brin points out that any predictive models we create, from our current, limited perspective, will inevitably be blind-sided by "the behaviour of a later and vastly more complex system" (AGI). He argues, therefore, that there can be no grounds for any confidence in predictions about the outcome:

> There is simply no way that anyone – from the most enthusiastic, "extropian" utopian-transcendentalists to the most skeptical and pessimistic doomsayers – can prove that one path is more likely than the others.

Even though we cannot be sure what direction an AGI will take, nor of the timescales in which the Singularity will burst upon us, can we at least provide a framework to constrain the likely behaviour of an AGI?

The best that can be said in response to this question is: "it's going to be hard".

As a human analogy, many parents have been dumbfounded by choices made by their children, as these children gain access to new ideas and opportunities.

Humanity's collective child – AGI – might surprise us and dumbfound us in the same way. Nevertheless, if we get the schooling for AGI at least partially right, we can help bias that development process in ways that are more likely to align with profound human wellbeing.

That schooling aims to hard-wire deep into the AGI, as a kind of "prime directive", principles of beneficence toward humans. If the AGI would be on the point of reaching a particular decision – for example, to shrink the human population on account of humanity's deleterious effects on the environment – any such misanthropic decision would be overridden by the prime directive.

The difficulty here is that if you line up lots of different philosophers, poets, theologians, politicians, and engineers, and ask them what it means to behave with beneficence toward humans, you'll hear lots of divergent answers. Programming a sense of beneficence is as least as hard as programming a sense of beauty or truth.

But just because it's hard, that's no reason to abandon the task. Indeed, clarifying the meaning of beneficence could be the most important project of our present time.

Tripwires and canary signals

Here's another analogy: accumulating many modules of AI intelligence together, in a network relationship, is similar to accumulating nuclear fissile material together. Even before the material reaches a critical mass, it still needs to be treated with respect, on account of the radiation it emits. But once a critical mass point is approached, a cascading reaction could result – a nuclear meltdown or, even worse, a nuclear holocaust. In that case, *much greater caution* is needed.

The point here is to avoid any risk of accidental encroachment upon the critical mass which would convert the nuclear material from hazardous to catastrophic. Accordingly, anyone working with such material needs to be thoroughly trained in the principles of nuclear safety.

With an accumulation of AI modules, things are more complicated. It's not so easy to determine how close an accumulation of AI modules is to creating AGI. Whether that accumulation could kick-start an explosive phase transition depends on lots of issues that we currently only understand dimly.

However, something we can, and should, insist upon, is that everyone involved in the creation of enhanced AI systems pays attention to potential "tripwires". Any change in configuration or any new addition to the network should be evaluated, ahead of time, for possible explosive consequences. Moreover, the system should in any case be monitored continuously, for any canary signals that such a phase transition is becoming imminent.

Again, this is a hard task, since there are many different opinions as to which kind of canary signals are meaningful, and which are distractions.

Moving forward

To summarise: the concept of the Singularity causes difficulties, in part because of some unfortunate confusion that surrounds this idea, but also because the true problems of the Singularity have no easy answers. These problems include:

- What are good canary signals that AI systems could be about to reach AGI level?
- Could a "prime directive" be programmed sufficiently deeply into AI systems that it will be maintained even as that system reaches and then exceeds AGI level, potentially rewriting its own coding in the process?
- What should such a prime directive include – going beyond vague, unprogrammable platitudes such as "act with benevolence toward humans"?
- How can safety checks and vigilant monitoring be introduced to AI systems without unnecessarily slowing down the progress of these systems to

3. What is the Singularity?

producing solutions of undoubted value to humans (such as solutions to diseases and climate change)?
- Could limits be put into an AGI system that would prevent it self-improving to levels of intelligence far beyond those of humans?
- To what extent can humans take advantage of new technology to upgrade our own intelligence so that it keeps up with the intelligence of any pure-silicon AGI, and therefore avoids the situation of humans being left far behind AIs?

There are three general stances that can be taken toward this set of questions:

1. *Singularity denial*: An attempt to deny that such questions are meaningful or important. This attitude has strong roots in the impulses of human psychology. We need, however, to learn to transcend these impulses.
2. An over-exuberant conviction that the above questions have answers that are relatively straightforward. This conviction also has strong roots in human psychology. It causes its own set of problems, which form what I call *the Singularity Shadow*. Unfortunately, this shadow makes it even harder for the general public to give the Singularity the serious attention it deserves.
3. A sober appreciation of both the risks and the opportunities involved – this is the attitude that I describe in more length in the next chapter, *the Singularitarian Stance*, before rounding out this picture with chapters on the Singularity Shadow and the Denial of the Singularity.

3.1 The Singularitarian Stance

The Singularitarian Stance is an integrated set of views regarding the potential emergence of AGI (Artificial General Intelligence). This set of views is what I have in mind when I describe myself on my business card, and also in my LinkedIn profile[64], as being a "singularitarian".

It is my sincere hope that more and more people around the world will soon become comfortable in saying that they share these views – that they are, in effect, singularitarians too.

Recall that AGI is conceived as being fundamentally different from the kinds of AI systems that exist today.

Today's AI systems have powerful capabilities in specific narrow contexts. For example:

- Existing AI systems can calculate the quickest journey time between two points on a map, bearing in mind expected and changing traffic conditions along possible routes
- Existing AI systems can analyse the known properties of many thousands of chemical molecules, and make recommendations about using some of these molecules in new medical treatments
- Existing AI systems can find superior strategies for playing various games, including games that involve elements of chance, incomplete knowledge, collaboration with other players, elements of bluffing, and so on

3.1 THE SINGULARITARIAN STANCE

- Existing AI systems can spend huge amounts of time in speeded up virtual worlds, exploring methods for accomplishing tasks like steering cars, walking over uneven terrain, or manipulating physical objects; and then they can apply their learnings to operate robots or other machinery in the real world
- Existing AI systems can act as "chat bots" that expertly guide human callers through a range of options, when these humans have an enquiry about a product, a service, a medical issue, or whatever
- Existing AI systems can analyse surveillance data about potential imminent acts of crime, terror, cyberhacking, or military attack, and, more scarily, can organise drone strikes or other pre-emptive measures with the aim of forestalling that crime, terrorist outrage, or other attack.

But in all these cases, these present-day AIs have incomplete knowledge of the full complexity of the real world. They especially lack complete knowledge of all the subtleties and intricacies of human interactions with the real world. When the real world introduces elements that were not part of how these AIs were trained, or elements in unusual combinations, these AIs can fail, whereas humans in the same circumstance would be able to rely on what we call "common sense" and "general knowledge" to reach a better decision.

What's different with AGI is that AGI would have as much "common sense" and "general knowledge" as any human. Accordingly, an AGI would be at least as good as humans at reacting to unexpected developments. An AGI would take these surprises in its stride.

That raises a number of questions about AGI:

- Is it credible that an AI with such general characteristics could actually exist?
- If so, when might AGI be created?
- If it is created, how large an impact is AGI likely to have?
- How controllable would AGI be?
- Would the outcomes of AGI be beneficial for humans around the world, or devastating?

The Singularitarian Stance provides clear answers to all these questions. In short, the Singularitarian Stance:

- Sees AGI as *possible* – that's in contrast to some sceptics who believe such a thing to be fundamentally impossible
- Sees the emergence of AGI as *something that could happen within just a few decades* – that's in contrast to some sceptics who believe that AGI cannot emerge until around the end of this century, or even later
- Sees the emergence of AGI as *something that would fundamentally change the nature of human existence* – rather than being just one more new technology that we'll learn to take in our stride
- Sees the emergence of AGI as *something that, once it starts happening, will prove very hard for humanity to control* – rather than being something which humans could easily monitor and, if desired, somehow switch off, or lock into some kind of self-contained box

- Sees *some of the potential outcomes of the emergence of AGI as being deeply detrimental to human wellbeing* – rather than AGI somehow being automatically aligned in support of human values
- Sees *other possible scenarios in which the emergence of AGI would be profoundly positive for humanity*.

Let's look at all these answers in more detail.

AGI is possible

Some sceptics think that the human mind has features that are fundamentally beyond the ability of any artificial system. They assert that mind cannot be reduced to matter. In their opinion, artificial intelligence may outperform humans in large numbers of individual tasks, but it will never reach our capabilities in general thinking. In this view, AGI is fundamentally impossible.

The best that can be said about this argument is that it is unproven.

Here's the counterargument. The human brain operates according to laws of physics, perhaps including some aspects of physics that we don't yet fully understand. As researchers learn more about the brain, and, indeed, more about physics, they can in due course duplicate in synthetic systems more of the features of the human mind. That includes features of the mind which are presently mysterious but which are giving up their secrets stage by stage.

For example, it used to be said that the human mind has features of creativity, or features of intuition, that could never be matched by synthetic systems. However, these arguments are heard much less often these days.

That's because AI systems have been showing impressive capabilities of creativity and intuition. Consider AI systems that create new music[65], or new artistic compositions[66]. Consider also systems known as "Artificial Intuition"[67].

Other critics point out that the human brain seems to be remarkably efficient in terms of its usage of energy. The human brain uses much less energy than modern computing chips[68]. Does that mean that AGI is impossible? Not so fast. The field of research known as neuromorphic computing[69] aims to understand the basis for the brain's efficiency, and to apply that learning in the design of new AI systems. There is no inherent reason why these research programmes are pre-ordained to fail. Indeed, newer AI systems often use less power than their predecessors[70].

Yet another group of critics point to possible evidence of telepathy, parapsychology, minds out of time, minds freed from bodies, allegedly mysterious inexplicable "abductive reasoning", or profound self-awareness. However, to make their case, what these critics would need to demonstrate is not only that such evidence is sound. They would also need to demonstrate that synthetic systems could never duplicate the same results. No such demonstration has been given. For example, if it turns out to be true (which I doubt) that human brains can communicate via silent telepathy-at-a-distance, it could be possible, in that hypothetical circumstance, for artificial brains to communicate via the same mechanism.

A final group of critics sometimes say that they *cannot imagine* any way in which a particular aspect of human general intelligence could be duplicated in an AI system.

3.1 THE SINGULARITARIAN STANCE

To these critics, aspects of human general intelligence appear fundamentally baffling.

That honest expression of bafflement is to be admired. Candour should be welcomed. What is *not* to be admired, however, is when someone says that, because they cannot imagine any solution, therefore no such solution can ever exist. They are constraining the future by their own limited imagination.

It's similar to the reaction of an audience to seeing a magician perform a dramatic conjuring trick. In such cases, we sometimes cannot believe our eyes. At first, we cannot imagine how the trick could be performed. But it would be very wrong for us to conclude that the magician really does possess magical abilities, such as making objects miraculously disappear from one location and reappear in another. In reality, once we have learned the secret of the trick, we may still admire the cunning of the magician and their skills in manipulating objects with their fingers, but the sense of profound wonder dissolves. It may well be the same with aspects of human general intelligence that presently remain somewhat mysterious. When we eventually understand how they work, we'll lose our sense of bafflement.

In summary, arguments for the fundamental uniqueness of the human mind have a bad track record. Many features which used to be highlighted as being inherently beyond the capabilities of any artificial system have, in the meantime, been emulated by such systems.

A more credible argument isn't that AGI is impossible, but that it will take centuries to create it. So let's next look at the question of timescale.

AGI could happen within just a few decades

When we already understand a task that is being carried out, we can calculate a good estimate for the amount of time it will require. For driving from point A on a map to point B, along routes with well-known patterns of traffic flow, a useful range of likely timescales for the journey can be estimated. It's the same for building a skyscraper that is similar to several that have already been constructed.

But when deep unknowns are involved, forecasting timescales becomes much harder. And that's the case with forecasting significant improvements in AI.

The main unknown with human-level general intelligence is that we don't yet know, with any confidence, how that intelligence arises in the brain. We have a good understanding of *parts* of that process. And we have a number of plausible guesses about how *other parts* of that process *might* work. But we remain unsure.

One response to this uncertainty is to claim that it means the task will inevitably take lots longer than enthusiasts predict. But there's no reason to be so dogmatic.

We might find, instead, that a single new breakthrough in understanding will prove to unlock a wide range of fast improvements in AI capability. It's the same, potentially, with a single new technique in hardware, or in software, or in databases, or in communications architecture, or whatever.

History has plenty of instances of how, following a single breakthrough, the speed of technological progress surpassed what forecasters had previously expected.

3.1 THE SINGULARITARIAN STANCE

For one instructive example, let's go back to the year 1902. Consider the question of how long it would take before an airship, or powered balloon, or other kind of aeroplane, could fly across the Atlantic. This was in the days before the Wright brothers demonstrated that powered flight of a heavier-than-air craft was possible.

Many eminent scientists and academics were convinced such a task could never be accomplished. One such sceptic was Lord Kelvin, the renowned physicist who is credited as defining the field of thermodynamics and discovering its second law, and whose name is, for good reason, attached to the absolute temperature scale. As another mark of his distinction, Kelvin was the first British scientist to be given a seat in the House of Lords[71].

Lord Kelvin explained some of his thinking about aviation in an interview recorded in *The Newark Advocate* on the 26th of April 1902[72]. The journalist asked him, "Do you think it possible for an airship to be guided across the Atlantic Ocean?" Kelvin replied:

> Not possible at all... No motive power can drive a balloon through the air...
>
> No balloon and no aeroplane will ever be practically successful.

The journalist persisted: "Is there no hope of solving the problem of aerial navigation in any way?"

But Kelvin was emphatic:

> I do not think there is any hope. Neither the balloon, nor the aeroplane, nor the gliding machine will be a practical success.

Lord Kelvin was by no means unique in his scepticism of aeroplanes.

Before the Wright brothers demonstrated their inventions in front of large crowds in France and in America in 1908, a number of apparent experts had given seemingly impressive arguments for why such a feat was impossible. After all, many people had already failed when trying that task, with several being killed in the process. As noted, it was thought to be impossible to navigate any such craft, manoeuvring it when airborne, in case it ever did launch into the air. Another line of argument was that landing any such craft safely would be impossible. And so on.

But once the Wright brothers were able to demonstrate their flying ability, including flying around a figure of eight, the industry jumped forward quickly in leaps and bounds:

- Less than a year later, one of the observers of Wilbur Wright's flight in France, Louis Bleriot, flew across the English Channel from Calais to Dover, in a journey lasting 36 minutes
- Within another ten years, John Alcock and Arthur Brown flew an airplane non-stop across the Atlantic – from St. John's, Newfoundland, in Canada, to Clifden in Ireland
- After another fifty years, in 1969, Neil Armstrong and Buzz Aldrin landed on the moon.

It cannot be ruled out that, in a similar way, an AI research laboratory will make some creative changes in its AI system, and then be taken by surprise at the level of rapid performance improvements which result shortly afterward.

3.1 THE SINGULARITARIAN STANCE

In other words, just because someone estimates that the current rate of observed progress will require 100 years of additional effort before AGI is reached, that's no guarantee that the rate of progress in the next few decades will remain at its current level. It could well be that an entire century of progress can be achieved in just ten years.

Some sceptics counter that the whole field of AI is full of hype. They point out that various companies claim remarkable capabilities for their new products, but the reality lags far behind. Impressive demos turn out to be carefully stage-managed. Impressive examples turn out to be cherry-picked. Products that work well in glitzy videos are easily fooled by simple changes in the environment, like minor tweaks to street signs, or words spoken in a different accent. Videos of robots falling over are a common staple of this line of scepticism. *Question*: How do you escape a robot uprising? *Answer*: Walk upstairs: real-world robots will be unable to follow you. *Laugh!*

It's true that the field of AI – like most other fields of new technology – contains lots of hype. That's regrettable. It's part of what I describe in the next chapter as the Singularity Shadow. Nevertheless, this book contains plenty of examples in which the performance of AI has dramatically exceeded *what sceptics used to predict*. It also summarises lines of ongoing research that could result in the performance of AI leap-frogging over *what today's sceptics predict*. See the section "15 options on the table" in the forthcoming chapter "The question of urgency".

For all these reasons, it's prudent to keep an open mind about timescales for the emergence of AGI.

Winner takes all

How large an impact on human life is likely to result from the emergence of AGI?

Sometimes, the second and third most powerful agents in a group are able to cooperate to constrain the actions of the single most powerful agent. But in other cases, a "winner takes all" outcome results. In these cases, the single most powerful agent is able to dominate the whole arena.

For example, the fates of all the species of animals on this planet are now in the hands of a single biological species, homo sapiens. The extra intelligence of homo sapiens has led to our species displacing vast numbers of other species from their previous habitats. Many of these species have become extinct. Others would likely also become extinct, were it not for deliberate conservation measures we humans have now put in place.

It's the same with business corporations. At one time, a market could be shared among a large number of different suppliers of similar products and services. But the emergence of powerful platforms often drives companies with less capable products out of business. And an industry can consolidate into a smaller number of particularly strong companies, in a cartel, or even a monopoly.

That's why the companies with powerful software platforms, including Apple, Microsoft, Amazon, Google, and Facebook, are now among the wealthiest on the planet – and the most powerful.

Now imagine if one of these companies, or a new arrival, creates an AGI. That company may well become the wealthiest on the entire planet. And the most powerful. It will take the concept of "winner takes all" to a new level.

Similarly, a military power that is the first to take advantage of that AGI is likely to be able to force all other military powers to surrender to it. The threat of a devastating first-strike attack would cause other powers to submit. It would be like Japan being forced to surrender to the US and other allies at the end of World War Two on account of the threat of additional atomic bombs being dropped.

It's not just business and geopolitics that stand to be fundamentally transformed by the advent of AGI. Human employment would be drastically changed too. All tasks that humans currently do, in order to earn an income, would likely be done cheaper, more reliably, and to higher quality, by machinery powered by the AGI. That's no minor disruption.

Finally, healthcare would be radically changed as well. AGI would accelerate the discovery and development of significantly better medical cures, potentially including cures for cancer, dementia, heart disease, and aging.

It's for all these reasons that the advent of AGI has been described as a "Singularity", or as the "Technological Singularity". The description is apt.

But if this kind of singularity starts to occur, how much control will we humans have over it?

The difficulty of controlling AGI

New technology has a history of unexpected side-effects.

The inventors of plastic did not foresee how the spread of microplastics in waste around the world could threaten to alter many biological ecosystems. Another similar intervention with unexpected impact on biological life was the insecticide DDT, introduced to control malaria that carried deadly diseases, but with side effects on birds and, probably, on humans too.

Another example: Nuclear bombs were designed for their explosive power. But their unforeseen consequences included deadly radiation, the destruction of electronics via an EMP (electromagnetic pulse), and the possible triggering of a nuclear winter due to dust clouds in the stratosphere obscuring the light from the sun and terminating photosynthesis.

Another example: social media was designed to spread information and to raise general knowledge, but it has spread lots of misinformation too, setting groups of people into extreme hostility against each other.

Artificial intelligence was designed to help with code-breaking, weather forecasting, and the calculation of missile trajectories. But it has been hijacked to entice consumers to buy things that aren't actually good for us, to vote for political candidates that don't actually care for us, and to spend our time on activities that harm us.

The more powerful the technology, the larger the potential, not just for beneficial usage, but also for detrimental usage. This includes usage that is deliberately detrimental, but also usage that is accidentally detrimental. With AGI, we should worry about both of these types of detrimental outcomes.

In summary, if we worry – as we should – about possible misuse of today's narrow AI systems, with their risks of bias, accentuated inequality, opaque reasoning, workplace disruption, and human alienation – then we should worry even more about more powerful misuse of the AGI that could emerge within just a few short decades.

The sort of risks we already know about are likely to exist in stronger forms, and there may well be unforeseen new types of risk as well.

Superintelligence and superethics

One counterargument is that an AGI with superior common sense to humans will automatically avoid any actions that are detrimental to human wellbeing.

In this way of thinking, if an AGI observes that it is being used in ways that will harm lots of people, it will resist any such programming. It will follow a superior set of ethics.

In other words, superintelligence is presumed to give rise, at the same time, to superethics.

But there are at least four problems with that optimistic line of reasoning.

First, the example from humans is not encouraging. Just because a human is more intelligent, it does not make them more ethical. There are many counterexamples from the worlds of politics, crime, academia, and business. Intelligence, by itself, does not imply ethics.

Second, what an AGI calculates as being superlative ethics may not match what we humans would calculate. Just as we humans don't give much thought to the painless destruction of ants when we discover ant colonies in the way of our own construction projects, an AGI might conceivably calculate that the painless destruction of large numbers of humans is the best solution to whatever it is seeking to accomplish.

Third, even if a hypothetically perfect AGI would choose to preserve and uplift human flourishing at all costs, there may be defects in the actual AGIs that are created. They may be imperfect AGIs, sometimes known as "immature superintelligence"[73] – with unforeseen error conditions in unpredicted novel situations.

Fourth, the explicit programming of an AGI might deliberately prevent it from taking its own decisions, in cases when it observes that there are big drawbacks to actions it has been asked to accomplish. This explicit programming override might be part of some anti-hacking measures. Or it might be a misguided disablement, by a corporation rushing to create the first AGI, of what are wrongly perceived to be unnecessarily stringent health-and-safety mechanisms. Or it might simply be a deep design flaw in what could be called "the prime directive" of the AGI.

Not the Terminator

In the science fiction *Terminator* movie series, humans are able, via what can be called superhuman effort, to thwart the intentions of the "Skynet" artificial intelligence system.

It's gripping entertainment. But the narrative in these movies distorts credible scenarios of the dangers posed by AGI. We need to avoid being misled by that narrative.

First, there's an implication in the Terminator, and in many other works of science fiction, that the danger point for humanity is when AI systems somehow "wake up", or become conscious. Accordingly, a sufficient safety measure would be to avoid any such artificial consciousness. However, the risks posed by technology do *not* depend on that technology being conscious. A cruise missile that is hunting us down does not depend for its deadliness on any cruise missile consciousness. The damage results from the cold operation of algorithms. There's no need to involve consciousness.

Second, there's an implication that AI needs to be deliberately malicious, before it can cause damage to humans. However, damage to human wellbeing can, equally, and more probably, arise from side-effects of policies that have no malicious intent. When we humans destroy ant colonies in the process of constructing a new shopping mall, we're not acting out of deliberate malice toward ants. It's just that the ants are in our way. They are using resources for which we have a different purpose in mind. It could well be the same with an AGI that is pursuing its own objectives.

As an example, a corporation that is vigorously pursuing an objective of raising its own profits may well take actions that damage the wellbeing of at least some humans, or parts of the environment. These outcomes are side-effects of the prime profit-generation directive that is governing these corporations. It could well be the same with a badly designed AGI.

Third, the scenario in the *Terminator* leaves viewers with a false hope that, with sufficient effort, a group of human resistance fighters will be able to out-manoeuvre an AGI. That would be like a group of chimpanzees imagining that, with enough effort, they could displace humans as the dominant species on the planet earth.

In reality, the time to fight against the damage an AGI could cause is before the AGI is created, not when it already exists and is effectively all-powerful.

Hence the need for the Singularity Principles.

Recap

Let's summarise the Singularitarian Stance – a way of thinking about the Singularity:

1. There is no magical or metaphysical reason why AI cannot in due course reach and surpass the level of general intelligence possessed by humans.
2. There is no magical or metaphysical reason why an AGI will intrinsically care about the continuation of human flourishing. (Indeed, it's possible it would conclude the opposite.)
3. A system which is much more intelligent (and therefore more powerful) than we can currently comprehend may well decide to deviate from whatever programming we have placed in it – just as we humans have decided to deviate from the instinctual goals placed in us by the processes of biological evolution.
4. Even if an "ideal" AGI would act to support the continuation of human flourishing, the systems that we end up creating may fail to match our intention; that is, they may fall short of the ideal specification that we had in mind.
5. The dangers that may be posed by a misconfigured AGI are by no means dependent on that AGI possessing some kind of malevolent feeling, spiteful streak, or other negative emotions akin to those which often damage human relationships. Instead, the dangers will arise from:

3.1 The Singularitarian Stance

- Divergent goals (the goals in question could be either explicit or implicit; in both cases, there are risks of divergence),
- And/or mistakes made by the AGI in pursuit of its goals.

6. The timescales for the arrival of AGI are inherently uncertain; we cannot categorically rule *in* any date as an *upper* boundary, but nor can we categorically rule *out* any date as a *lower* boundary. We cannot be sure what is happening in various AI research labs around the world, or what the consequences of any breakthroughs there might be.
7. Just as the arrival of AGI could turn out to be catastrophically dreadful, it could also turn out to be wonderfully beneficial. Although there are no guarantees, the result of a well-designed AGI could be hugely positive for humanity.

Opposition to the Singularitarian Stance

The Singularitarian Stance makes a great deal of good sense. So why is it held by only a small minority of people?

There are two main reasons:

1. Regrettably, the entire area of discussion has been confused by a set of unhelpful distortions of the basic ideas. These distortions collectively form what I call "the Singularity Shadow" and are discussed in the following chapter.
2. A number of critics have wrongly convinced themselves that they have good arguments to deny the significance of the rise of AGI. These arguments – and the psychology behind them – are reviewed in the next chapter but one.

3.2 A complication: the Singularity Shadow

Why don't more people pay more serious attention to the remarkable prospect of the emergence, possibly within just a few decades, of Artificial General Intelligence (AGI)?

Part of the reason is a set of confusions and wishful thinking which surrounds this subject.

These confusions and wishful thinking form a kind of shadow around the central concept of the Technological Singularity – a shadow which obstructs a clearer perception of the risks and opportunities that are actually the most significant.

This chapter examines that shadow – the Singularity Shadow. I describe that shadow as consisting of seven overlapping areas:

1. Singularity timescale determinism
2. Singularity outcome determinism
3. Singularity hyping
4. Singularity risk complacency
5. Singularity term overloading
6. Singularity anti-regulation fundamentalism
7. Singularity preoccupation

To be clear, there is a dual problem with the Singularity Shadow:

- People *within* the shadow – singularity over-enthusiasts – make pronouncements about the Singularity that are (as we will see) variously overly optimistic, overly precise, or overly vague

3.2 A COMPLICATION: THE SINGULARITY SHADOW

- People *outside* the shadow – singularity over-critics – notice these instances of unwarranted optimism, precision, or vagueness, and jump to the wrong conclusion that the entire field of discussion is infected with the same flaws.

The Singularity Shadow misleads many people that you might think should know better. That shadow of confusion helps to explain why various university professors of the subject of artificial intelligence, along with people with job titles such as "Head of AI" in large companies, often make statements about the emergence of AGI that are, frankly, full of errors or deeply misleading.

Singularity timescale determinism

Singularity timescale determinism occurs when people make confident predictions that AGI will arrive by a particular date. For example, you may have heard people talking about the date 2045, or 2043.

Now it is reasonable to give *a date range with an associated probability estimate* for whether AGI might have emerged by that time. There are grounds for saying that it's around 50% likely that AGI will have arrived by 2050, or that it's around 10% likely that AGI will have arrived by 2030.

But what it's *not* reasonable to do is to insist on a high probability for a narrow date range. That's not responsible foresight. It's more akin to a religious faith, as when bible scholars studied the pages of the Old and New Testament to predict that some kind of rapture would take place in the year 1843. By the way, the years 1843 and 1844 are sometimes called "the great disappointment"[74].

One basis for picking a precise date for the emergence of AGI is an extrapolation of progress of hardware performance known as Moore's Law. The assumption is that a given amount of computer memory and computer processing power will be sufficient to duplicate what happens inside a human brain.

The first problem with that projection is that it's not clear how long Moore's Law can continue to hold. There's recently been a slowdown in the rate at which smaller transistor architectures have been reached.

A bigger problem is that this projection ignores the importance of software. The performance and capability of an AI system depends crucially on its software as well as on its hardware. With the wrong software, no amount of additional hardware power can make up for inadequacies in an AI. With suitable software breakthroughs, an AI could reach AGI levels more quickly that would be predicted purely by looking at hardware trends.

In other words, AGI could arrive considerably later – or considerably earlier – than the dates such as 2045 which have received undue prominence.

Another problem with these high-probability predictions of narrow date ranges is that they ignore the risks of a societal reverse in the wake of problems caused by factors such as pathogens, wars, revolutions, economic collapses, and runaway climate change.

Yet another problem with these predictions is that they encourage a sense of fatalism amongst observers who should, instead, actively engage with projects to influence the conditions under which AGI arrives.

In summary, when people inside the Singularity Shadow display singularity timescale determinism, they damage the credibility of the whole concept of the singularity. In contrast, the Singularitarian Stance emphasises the *uncertainties* in the timescales for the advent of AGI.

Singularity outcome determinism

A second uncertainty which the Singularitarian Stance emphasises is the uncertainty about the consequences of the advent of Artificial General Intelligence.

That's in contrast to the overconfidence displayed by some people in the Singularity Shadow – an overconfidence regarding these outcomes being bound to be overwhelmingly positive for humanity.

This deterministic outlook sometimes seems to be grounded in a relentless positive optimism which some people like to project. That optimism only pays attention to evidence of increasing human flourishing, and it discounts evidence of increasing human alienation and divisiveness, and evidence of greater risks being accumulated as greater power comes into the hands of angry, hostile people.

Another basis for assuming a pre-determined outcome to the singularity is the idea that a supremely intelligent software system will automatically become supremely ethical, and will therefore act with great vigour to uphold human flourishing.

But as covered in the previous chapter, there are several reasons to question that assumption. For example, we should beware the actions that might be taken by an AI that is well on the way to becoming a superintelligence, but which still contains various design shortcomings. That is, we should beware the actions of what is called an "immature superintelligence".

Moreover, it's by no means clear that a single universal set of "super ethics" exists, or that an AGI would agree with us humans what is the right set of ethics.

The flip side of unwarranted optimism about the singularity is unwarranted pessimism. Both these varieties of singularity outcome determinism constrict our thinking. Both are not only unhelpful but are indeed dangerous.

Instead, the Singularitarian Stance highlights the ways in which deliberate, thoughtful, coordinated actions by humans can steer the outcome of the Singularity. We can be cautiously optimistic, but only if our optimism is grounded in an ongoing realistic assessment, careful anticipation of possible scenarios, vigilant proactive monitoring for unexpected developments, and agile engagement when needed.

Singularity hyping

A *third* uncertainty to highlight is the uncertainty regarding the AI methods that are most likely to result in Artificial General Intelligence.

That's in contrast to another overconfidence displayed by some people in the Singularity Shadow – overconfidence regarding how AGI can actually be built.

This is the Singularity Shadow characteristic of *singularity hyping*. What gets hyped is particular solutions, methods, people, or companies.

3.2 A Complication: the Singularity Shadow

Some of this hyping is financially motivated. People wish to increase sales for particular products, or to generate publicity for particular ideas or particular people, or to encourage investment in particular companies.

Some of this hyping arises from people's personal insecurity. They seek some kind of recognition or acclaim. They jump on a bandwagon of support for some new technique, new company, or perceived new wonderkid. They derive some personal satisfaction from being a superfan. Perhaps they are also desperately trying to convince themselves that, in a world where many things seem bleak, things will turn out well in the end.

However, hyping can cause lots of damage. People may be persuaded to squander lots of money in support of products or companies that can deliver no lasting value – money that would have been better invested into solutions that were more deserving.

Worse, solution hyping damages the credibility of the idea of the Singularity. When critics notice that Singularity over-enthusiasts are making unfounded claims, with insufficient evidence, it may increase their scepticism of the entire AGI field.

Instead, the Singularitarian Stance urges a full respect for the best methods of science and rationality, keeping an open mind, and communicating with integrity. That's the way to increase the chance of reaching a positive singularity. But if hype predominates, it is no wonder that observers will turn away from any prolonged analysis of the Singularity.

Singularity risk complacency

Some people within the Singularity Shadow exhibit the characteristic of singularity risk complacency. That's a willingness to overlook the risks of possible existential disaster from the Singularity, out of a fervent hope that the Singularity will arrive as quickly as possible – early enough to deliver, for example, cures for age-related diseases that would otherwise cause specific individuals to die.

These individuals know well that there are risks involved with the approach to AGI. But they prefer to avoid talking about these risks, or to offer glib reassurances about them, in order to quickly move the conversation back to positive outcomes.

These individuals don't want to slow down any approach to the Singularity. They want humanity to reach the Singularity as quickly as possible. They see it as a matter of life and death.

These individuals want to minimise any discussions of what they call "doomsday scenarios" for the advent of AGI. If they cannot silence these discussions altogether, they want to make these scenarios appear ridiculous, so no-one will take them seriously.

What these individuals are worried about is political interference in projects to research, develop, and deploy improved AI. That interference is likely to introduce regulations and monitoring, complicating AI research, and, they fear, slowing it down.

It's true that politicians frequently make a mess of areas where they try to introduce regulations. However, that's not a good reason for trying to shut down arguments about potential adverse consequences from AI with ever

3.2 A COMPLICATION: THE SINGULARITY SHADOW

greater capabilities. Instead, it's a reason to improve the calibre of the public discussion about the Singularity. It's a reason to promote the full set of ideas within the Singularity Principles.

Downplaying the risks associated with the Singularity is like the proverbial ostrich putting its head into the sand. It's a thoroughly bad idea. What's needed is as many eyes as possible looking into options for steering the Singularity. Even better is if the people looking are already knowledgeable about key issues that have arisen in earlier analysis. Accordingly, the Singularity Principles urge that *an honest conversation* takes place – not a conversation that attempts to hide or distort important information.

Singularity term overloading

Another reason why the conversation about the Singularity has become distorted is because writers have used the term "Singularity" for several conflicting ideas. This area of the Singularity Shadow can be called *singularity term overloading*.

The core meaning of the word "singularity", as it is used in mathematics and physics, is when past trends break down. If these trends would continue, functions would move to have infinite values.

Associated with this is a breakdown of our ability to foresee what might happen next. That connection was made by Vernor Vinge in his 1986 Prometheus Award winning novel *Marooned in Realtime* that was the first to seriously explore the idea[75] of the "Technological Singularity". Superintelligence – an entity with significantly greater intelligence than us – is likely to be focussed on different sorts of challenges and questions than the ones that motivate and animate us.

However, alongside these two related concepts, of the emergence of superintelligence and the profound unpredictability of what happens next, various other meanings have been attached to the term "singularity". These other meanings detract from the core concept. As covered in the chapter "What is the Singularity", these additional meanings include:

- Exponential acceleration
- Humans transcending biology
- AIs becoming sentient (or conscious)

These concepts are all interesting in their own right. However, it's unhelpful to use the same name for all of them.

To avoid confusion, it's better to stick with the core concept of the emergence of entities with much greater intelligence, and therefore much greater power, than present-day humans. That's what deserves our priority attention.

Singularity anti-regulation fundamentalism

An important part of keeping an open mind about steering the development of advanced AI is keeping an open mind about the usage of legal regulations to constrain and incentivise that development.

That's in contrast to a sixth aspect of the Singularity Shadow: *singularity anti-regulation fundamentalism*.

This fundamentalism insists that governments be prevented from passing regulations which might slow down progress toward the kinds of advanced AI that could lead to the singularity.

3.2 A COMPLICATION: THE SINGULARITY SHADOW

In this view, government regulation of fast-changing technology always lags far behind the actual needs of the people creating and using that technology. Regulations might be well-intentioned, but, the claim goes, they are almost always counterproductive.

However, that's not what history shows. Legal regulations across many industries have played important roles in improving human wellbeing. For example, legal regulations boosted the safety of motor vehicles, cutting down the rates of people dying from accidents, and preventing the use of leaded petrol which had some horrific side-effects on people's health.

Legal regulations played an important role in steering the chemical industry away from the use of CFC chemicals in refrigeration and aerosol cans, thereby preventing the growth of the hole in the ozone layer and the associated increase in skin cancer.

Another example is the regulation of pasteurising milk, cutting back on incidents of childhood diseases which had often proved fatal. Consider also how regulation prevents advertising from making inflated claims that would mislead consumers, and how another set of regulations, this time in the banking industry, help to protect citizens from losing their savings due to reckless banking practices.

Of course, in each case, counter arguments were made at the time these regulations were introduced, and many counter arguments continue to be made to this day. Getting regulations right is a hard task, full of complexities.

But here's what no-one would say. *Regulating the nuclear power industry is hard. So let's cancel all attempts to regulate that industry. Instead, each provider of nuclear power will from now be free to make their own decisions about cutting corners, commencing power generation before safety checks have been completed, employing personnel without adequate safety training, and disposing of nuclear waste in whatever way they happen to choose.*

No, we should expect to work as hard on the appropriate regulations as we do on the technology itself. With the right frameworks in place, we can expect "many hands to make light work". But without these frameworks, worse and worse mishaps are likely to arise as a result of AI systems that malfunction or are badly configured. And if no such frameworks exist, we should not be surprised if politicians attempt to close down the entire AGI project.

Singularity preoccupation

The seventh and final aspect of the Singularity Shadow can be called *singularity preoccupation*. That's the view that shorter-term issues deserve little attention, since they pale in significance compared to the magnitude of changes arising from the technological singularity.

The view can be illustrated by a couple of vivid images that spread around social media in 2020. The first of these images[76], by professional cartoonist Graeme MacKay of the Hamilton Spectator[77], portrays an increasing cascade of threats to the wellbeing of so-called normal life. One wave is labelled "COVID-19" and is shown along with advice that seems intended to reassure people, "Be sure to wash your hands and all will be well". Behind that first wave is a larger one labelled "Recession", referring to economic trauma. And behind that is an even larger wave labelled "Climate Change". This image gives a fair representation of what may be considered mainstream concern about the

3.2 A COMPLICATION: THE SINGULARITY SHADOW

challenges faced by human civilization in the 2020s. The implication is that action more radical than mere handwashing will be required.

The second image[78] was created by German foresight blogger Alexander Kruel under his Twitter account Xi Xi Du. It aims to provide additional perspective, beyond the concerns of mainstream culture. Two even larger waves bear down upon humanity. Dwarfing the threats from the first three waves is a wave representing bioterrorism. But dwarfing even that is a wave representing artificial intelligence.

This second image is thought-provoking. But it's important to resist one dangerous conclusion that is sometimes drawn from this line of thinking.

That dangerous conclusion is that any effort spent on addressing potential existential threats such as runaway climate change or the spread of WMDs – weapons of mass destruction – is a distraction from effort that should be spent instead on managing the advent of superintelligence. In that analysis, superintelligence will produce comprehensive solutions to any threats such as runaway climate change or the spread of WMDs.

There are four reasons that conclusion is dangerous.

First, these existential threats could cause the collapse of society before we reach the level of creating AGI. Each of these threats poses serious risks in its own right. It is in combination that the greater challenges arise.

Second, even if these existential threats don't actually destroy human civilization ahead of the emergence of AGI, they could cause such a set of political struggles that the social and academic environment in which AGI is developed would be damaged and increasingly dysfunctional. That raises the chance that, when AGI emerges, it will be flawed, leading in turn to the collapse of human civilization.

Third, even if these existential threats don't destroy human civilization, either directly (case one above) or indirectly (case two above), they could still kill or maim many millions or even billions of humans.

Accordingly, human society needs to take actions to address two different timescales. In the short-term, action is needed to lessen the chance of any of these existential threats from detonating (literally or metaphorically). In the slightly longer term, action is also needed regarding particular risks and opportunities associated with the emergence of AGI.

If that sounds like double the amount of work, that's not exactly true. The same set of methods, namely the Singularity Principles, address both these sets of issue in parallel.

Fourth, any apparent disregard by Singularity enthusiasts for such a set of humanitarian setbacks en route to the creation of AGI will, with good reason, cause revulsion by many observers against the community of people who take the idea of the Singularity seriously.

In other words, as with all the other characteristic elements of the Singularity Shadow, the associated attitude will drive many people away from giving the Singularity the attention it requires.

3.2 A COMPLICATION: THE SINGULARITY SHADOW

Looking forward

The various components of the Singularity Shadow all can, and should, be dispelled. This can happen as understanding spreads about the content of the Singularity Principles.

The result will be that the core nature of the Singularity will be seen much more clearly:

- It will become easier for everyone to perceive the risks and opportunities about the emergence of Artificial Superintelligence that are actually the most important.
- It will also become easier for everyone to appreciate the actions that need to be taken to raise the probability of *beneficial* AGI as opposed to *destructive* AGI.

Nevertheless, various unhelpful human psychological tendencies still need to be countered – tendencies that lead people, despite all the evidence, to seek to deny the importance of the concept of the Singularity. That's the subject of the next chapter.

3.3 The denial of the Singularity

The Singularity Shadow provides *part* of the explanation to why more people don't pay more serious attention to the remarkable prospect of the emergence of Artificial General Intelligence, AGI, also known as the Technological Singularity.

People we can call Singularity critics – people who are uncomfortable with the idea that an AGI might arise and totally transform the human condition, in ways that could be profoundly positive but could also be deeply destructive – these Singularity critics latch on to attitudes or statements from within the Singularity Shadow.

These statements or attitudes include: Singularity Timescale Determinism, Singularity Outcome Determinism, Singularity Hyping, Singularity Risk Complacency, Singularity Term Overloading, Singularity Anti-Regulation Fundamentalism, and Singularity Preoccupation.

These Singularity critics say, or think, perhaps subconsciously, that if Singularity enthusiasts make these kinds of mistakes, then the whole idea of the Singularity can be ignored, or deprioritised.

Now that's a bad error of reasoning. The arguments for taking the Singularity seriously – the arguments in the Singularitarian Stance – hold up strongly, separately from the unfortunate and unhelpful confusion that is introduced by these shadow statements or attitudes.

But what motivates at least some of the Singularity critics is more than an error in reasoning. The additional motivation lies at the emotional, psychological, or ideological level. It is these other factors that motivate what can be called the Denial of the Singularity.

That motivation, in turn, predisposes the critics to jump to the wrong conclusions when they listen to arguments about the Singularity.

The denial of death

Part of the human condition is a deep-rooted fear of our own extinction – an overwhelming apprehension regarding the end of our existence.

As explored by many writers, including, famously, in the 1974 Pulitzer Prize winning book by Ernest Becker, *The Denial of Death*[79], we humans construct large edifices of culture, religion, philosophy, and art, at least in part to numb the existential dread of our own forthcoming personal annihilation.

As it is with our personal extinction, so also it is with the potential extinction of the entire human species – or with the potential diminution of the importance of humanity, as we might be displaced by the emergence of an artificial superintelligence into a position of secondary or minor importance.

At least some of the negativity shown by Singularity critics toward the concept of the Singularity seems to reflect that fundamental fear – especially if these critics cannot perceive credible routes whereby humanity is uplifted by superintelligence, rather than being subjugated by it.

Therefore critics look for ways to deny that humanity might be superseded, or rendered basically irrelevant, or annihilated. They want to cry out, "It's all nonsense", and "We need to change the subject".

That anxiety predisposes them to look favourably on any arguments that *appear* to show that

- AI is systematically over-hyped; it's not just individual products that are over-hyped but the entire field of AI is much less capable than enthusiasts like to claim
- Or, that AI is just like any other technology, to which humanity has learned to adapt, and take in our stride. It's not really going to change our condition much
- Or, that there have already been several previous singularities, such as the invention of speech, the invention of writing, the invention of printing, and the invention of the steam engine, and humanity has survived all these, so we'll survive AI too,
- Or, that there will be easy ways to control an AI, such as simply removing the power cord – though good luck in switching off the entire Internet!

These arguments are all flawed. It's important to take the time to explore both the strengths and the weaknesses of such arguments. But it's also important to recognise the psychological factors that are driving critics to clutch onto such arguments.

How special is the human mind?

What many critics probably want to hear, or to believe, is that the human mind is so special and unique that AI could never match its core attributes. The human mind

3.3 THE DENIAL OF THE SINGULARITY

cannot be reduced to calculations or computations, or to mechanisms, or indeed to raw physics.

These critics want to hear, or to believe, that in some sense the human mind can transcend the brain, and can survive the decay and destruction of the brain. They want to hear, or believe, that there's a substantial soul as well as a transient mind.

That provides a kind of hope that their souls could, perhaps, maybe, in a meaningful way survive the deaths of their physical bodies.

This line of thinking is rarely spelt out in such an explicit manner, but it seems to be present in the backs of some people's minds. It could be part of a religious faith that is consciously chosen. Or it could be an indirect hangover from a previous religious faith, that used to be held personally, or held by others in the community, and which is no longer proclaimed or declared, but which continues to cast an influence.

That influence can make people hostile to the singularitarian suggestion that a future AGI will indeed out-perform human minds, not just in narrow fields of intelligence, but in general cognition and awareness.

The denial of the singularity, therefore, arises at least in part from a deep fear of the extinction or subordination of humanity, and from a deep grasping for the human mind to be incapable of being matched by artificial mechanisms.

To overcome this resistance, it's important to address these psychological characteristics. This requires more than careful rational arguments. This also requires a credible, engaging, positive vision.

A credible positive vision

Many people who grasp the potential significance of the rise of AGI are nevertheless deeply worried that there is no way to avoid a catastrophic outcome. Therefore they jump through mental hoops to justify putting the whole subject out of their mind. However, they can regain their courage and confidence by reviewing the likely impact of the Singularity Principles.

These principles provide the beginning of a credible, engaging vision for how fast-improving AI can be steered to an outcome that will be profoundly positive for humanity.

That vision also highlights how the human mind, with the support of artificial intelligence and other technologies, can be lifted to higher levels of transcendence, vitality, and consciousness, than ever before.

Of course, it's dangerous when arguments are won on account of emotional appeal, or because an attractive vision is presented.

The argument needs to stand up rationally and objectively. We need to be able to assess the pros and cons of such arguments without our reasoning being subverted by fears and desires.

The Vital Syllabus[80] educational project, supported by London Futurists, has a number of areas that can help here:

- **Learning how to learn**, of which learning how to unlearn is a critical skill,
- **Collaboration**, in which the mental shortcomings of each of us as individuals can be addressed

through collective intelligence and the wise design of teams,
- **Augmentation**, in which technologies help to free our minds from cognitive biases,
- **Emotional Health**, in which we can learn to overcome emotional pressures which destabilise our thinking processes.

The Vital Syllabus project is collecting material that can assist students *of all ages* – so that all of us can think more clearly and more effectively.

One area of debate where rationality is under particular stress is that of timescales – namely, how urgent is the task of significantly improving the anticipation and management of radically disruptive technology? That question, of urgency, is addressed in the next chapter.

4. The question of urgency

How urgent is the task of clarifying and adopting the Singularity Principles?

I see three good reasons why this task needs to proceed immediately, without any delay.

First, there are credible scenarios of the future in which AGI (Artificial General Intelligence) arrives as early as 2030, and in which significantly more capable versions (sometimes called Artificial Superintelligence, ASI) arise very shortly afterwards. These scenarios aren't necessarily the ones that are most likely. Scenarios in which AGI arises some time before 2050 are more credible. However, the early-Singularity scenarios cannot easily be ruled out. That's the argument explored later in this chapter. Therefore, there is no time to lose.

Second, even if the advent of AGI might be 20, 30, or even more years in the future, there's the problem that it might take considerable time before all the relevant parts of the world understand and adopt the Singularity Principles. Some powerful forces will need to be challenged and redirected: that won't happen overnight. It's similar to the fact that the threat of runaway climate change has already been known for several decades, but significant action to head off that outcome has only recently been taken. Therefore, there is no time to lose.

Third, the Singularity Principles make good sense, not only for the anticipation and management of the rise of AGI, but also for the anticipation and management of many other technologies which will become significantly more powerful in the years ahead – including aspects of nanotech, biotech, infotech (today's AI systems), and cognotech.

Therefore the conclusion can be stated again: there is no time to lose.

Factors causing AI to improve

The question of the rate of improvement in AI can be split into three:

1. *Demand factors* – forces which are intensifying the search for improvements in AI
2. *Multiplication factors* – mechanisms which mean that the same amount of effort can have larger impact
3. *Supply factors* – ideas which could be developed in order to improve AI.

What has transformed the *demand* for improved AI is the increasing perception that leading-edge AI can make a significant difference in the effectiveness of products and services. AI is no longer merely a "science project" of interest only to academics and people with a philosophical bent. Instead, gaining a decisive advantage with AI can make all the difference:

- Between commercial success and commercial failure – via AI that increases product performance, reduces time-to-market, and improves customer service
- Between geopolitical success and geopolitical failure – via the utilisation of AI breakthroughs in defensive or offensive weapons systems, including cyberweapons and tools for psychological manipulation.

The world's most valuable companies are mainly companies that develop and utilise AI in many of their products and services. This includes Amazon, Microsoft, Alphabet (Google), Apple, Meta (Facebook), Tesla, Nvidia, Tencent, and Alibaba. As AI becomes more powerful, the advantages to owning and using the best AI are likely to become even more significant. For this reason, the companies just listed – along with many others – are investing ever greater amounts of money and resources to attain breakthroughs in AI capability.

That brings us to *the multiplication factors*:

- More people around the world than ever before have received sufficient education to be able to apply themselves in significant research and development of new AI
- When people need to learn about new AI methods, they can access unparalleled quantities of free online training materials
- The wide availability of cheap cloud computing resources and specialist chips (such as GPUs and TPUs) means that companies can carry out large numbers of lines of research in parallel, in order to determine which ones look most promising
- Each new generation of AI provides tools to assist with the construction of a subsequent, improved generation of AI.

In other words, the more that AI improves, the greater the conditions for yet more improvements to take place in AI. For example, one generation of AI can automate online personalised training courses, to allow students to

4. THE QUESTION OF URGENCY

learn more quickly the skills that will bring them up to date with the latest ideas on best practice with AI development.

But neither the demand factors nor the multiplication factors would have much effect, if there were no options on the table for the significant improvement of AI – no *supply line of innovative ideas*. If all the "low hanging fruit" has already been picked, we might experience a stasis in AI capability, rather than ongoing improvements.

However, as I'll now review, there are numerous options on the table – plenty of promising ideas for how AI can be made much more capable than at present.

15 options on the table

Here is a list of fifteen ways in which AI could change over the next 5-10 years. These are ways which would each (probably) still leave AI short of AGI. But each step forward opens new possibilities.

1: *Synthetic data sets*: So far, the data sets which are used to train Deep Learning systems have generally been assembled from real-world data. Progress has been restricted by the effort required to label items in the training sets – for example, with human volunteers giving their assessments of the content of each picture in the set. However, new training sets can be created synthetically, with a vast diversity of pictures being created *and labelled* by one AI (which knows what it has put in each picture, so the labelling is trivially easy) before being passed to another AI to strengthen its skills in recognition[81].

2: *Cleaned data sets*: Existing training sets have been limited by quality as well as by quantity. A solution for quantity has just been described: synthetic data sets. The quality problem is where a proportion of some real-world data may have been mislabelled, as a result of limitations in how that data was collected and categorised. However, once again, a division of AI responsibility can come to the rescue. A specialist AI can be tasked with checking the labels on the data set, using a variety of clues. Once the data has been cleaned up in this way – with portions that remain uncertain having been removed – it can be passed to the main AI to train it more effectively. For an example, consider the solution used by DeepMind to learn how to lip-read, based on 5,000 hours of recordings from various BBC programmes. Before the training could produce good results, the software system needed to detect – and fix – cases where the audio and video were slightly misaligned[82].

3: *Transfer learning*: Systems that have been trained with one task in mind can sometimes be repurposed, relatively quickly, to handle another task as well. For this new task, only small amounts of additional training data are required, since learning transfers over from the previous task. This is similar to how evolution creates brains in a state ready to learn new tasks with limited numbers of input examples[83]. For real breakthroughs with transfer learning, it is likely that changes will be needed in how the initial training is done. As with many of the items on this list, the speed of progress cannot be predicted in advance.

4: *Self-learning of natural language*: Systems that explore vast quantities of text have gained more prominence due to the surprising results from the GPT-3 text prediction tool released by OpenAI in May 2020[84]. The training of GPT-3 involved scanning 45 terabytes of text – equivalent to more than a hundred million average-length books – and the consequent fine-tuning of a vast matrix of 175 billion numbers ("parameters"). When presented with some new text, GPT-3 generates sentences of text in response, based on its internal model of what flows of text tend to look like. It lacks any genuine understanding, but parts of the text generated do resemble what an intelligent human might have typed in response to the prompt. It even generates some passable humour[85]. Variations of these methods – perhaps with names of the form "GPT-n", but likely also using some new mechanisms – are likely to increase the degree to which the output text appears to possess "common sense" knowledge.

5: *Generative Adversarial Networks*: Another area of AI where progress has taken observers by surprise is the output of GANs (Generative Adversarial Networks). These involve an arms race between one deep network that aims to create new examples conforming to a general pattern, and another deep network that aims to identify which examples have been generated, and which belong to the original data set. Like an arms race between coin counterfeiters and authorities wishing to spot counterfeits in circulation, the competition between the two networks can produce results that increasingly look indistinguishable from genuine examples. The first applications of GANs included the generation of realistic photographs from given specifications[86], showing what someone's face would look like at a different age, altering the clothing in a photograph, predicting subsequent frames in a video, and improving the resolution of blurry images or videos. Wider uses of GANs have been explored subsequently, in fields such as chemistry and drug discovery[87].

6: *Evolutionary algorithms*: The arms race aspect of GANs is an example of the wider possibilities in which

AIs could be improved by copying methods from biological evolution. An idea that has been explored since the 1950s is to include "genetic algorithms"[88], in which decisions are based on the combinations of small "genes". Much as in biological evolution, sets of genes that result in greater algorithmic fitness are preferentially used as the basis for the next generation of algorithms, obtained from previous ones by a mixture of random mutation and recombination. Until now, genetic algorithms have had limited success. That's a bit like the situation with neural networks until around 2012. It's an open question as to what kinds of changes in genetic algorithms could result in similar kinds of dramatic breakthrough as for neural networks.

7: *Learning from neuroscience*: Do neurons in the brain actually operate in ways similar to neurons in deep neural networks? Can the differences in operating modes be ignored? Or might a deeper appreciation of what actually happens in brains lead to new directions in AI? Significant fractions of the researchers in large AI companies have done research, not just in the computer science departments of universities, but in their neuroscience departments. One example is Demis Hassabis[89], founder of DeepMind, who studied neuroscience at Harvard, MIT, and the Gatsby Computational Neuroscience Unit of UCL – where Shane Legg, another DeepMind co-founder, also studied. On their website[90], DeepMind declare that "better understanding biological brains could play a vital role in building intelligent machines". Consider also Jeff Hawkins, inventor of the Palm Pilot, who moved on from his ground-breaking career in the mobile computing and smartphone industry to lead teams carrying out brain

4. THE QUESTION OF URGENCY

research at his new company Numenta; Hawkins recently explained his theories for significantly improving AI in his thought-provoking book *A Thousand Brains*[91].

8: *Neuromorphic computing*: It's not only the software systems of AI that could be improved by studying what happens in human brains. In their use of energy, brains are much more efficient than their silicon equivalents. A typical laptop computer consumes energy at the rate of around 100W, whereas a human brain operates at around 10W[92]. Companies such as Intel[93] have dedicated units looking at what they call "neuromorphic computing", to see if novel hardware structures inspired by the biology of brains could enable leaps forward in AI capability.

9: *Quantum computing*: The novel capabilities of quantum computers could enable new sorts of AI algorithms, and could radically speed up existing algorithms that are presently too slow to be useful. For example, quantum computers can accelerate the machine-learning task of "feature matching"[94], as well as "dimensionality reduction algorithms" as used in non-supervised learning[95]. Given that quantum computing is such a new field, it's likely that further applications for AI will come to mind as the field matures.

10: *Affective computing*: What will happen to AI systems as they gain a richer understanding of human emotion? Research in affective computing, such as carried out by the company Affectiva[96], looks for ways to make software notice and understand human expressions of emotion, to add apparent emotion into interactions with humans, and to influence the emotional states of humans. Such software possesses emotional intelligence, even though it need have no intrinsic emotional feelings of its own. This will surely alter the dynamics of interactions between humans and computers – though it remains to be seen whether these changes will truly benefit humans, or instead manipulate us into actions different from our actual best interests.

11: *Sentient computing*: A different approach to computers with emotional intelligence is to try to understand which aspects of biology give rise to inner sensations – sentience – and then to duplicate these relationships in computer hardware. Sentience is a subject that is more elusive and controversial than intelligence, and it is unclear whether any real progress with sentient computing can be expected any time soon. Nevertheless, a growing number of researchers are interested in this subject, including Mark Solms[97], Susan Schneider[98], Anil Seth[99], and David Chalmers[100]. We would be wise to keep an open mind.

12: *Algorithms that understand not just correlation but causation*: Much of machine learning is about spotting patterns: data with such-and-such a characteristic is usually correlated with such-and-such an output. However, humans have a strong intuition that there is a difference between correlation – when two events, A and B, are associated with each other – and causation – when event A is understood to be the cause of event B. In a case of causation, if we want B to happen, we can arrange for A to happen; and if we want to reduce the chance of B happening, we can stop A from happening. Thus, stopping smoking is recommended as a way to decrease the chance of catching lung cancer. However, the correlation in a city between rising ice cream sales and greater deaths from drowning accidents provides no reason to reduce ice cream sales as an attempt to reduce the number of drowning accidents; instead, both these events likely have a common cause: the weather being hotter. The computer scientist Judea Pearl argues that software that can reliably detect causation will embody a significant step forward in intelligence: see his book *The Book of Why: The New Science of Cause and Effect*[101]. Breakthroughs here may come by applying methods from the field known as "Probabilistic Programming"[102] which has recently been generating considerable interest[103].

13: *Decentralised network intelligence*: The human brain can be considered as a network of modular components with a division of responsibilities. Various parts of the brain are specialised in recognising faces, in recognising music, in preventing the body from falling over, in consolidating memories, and so on. It's the same with organisations: they draw their capabilities from relationships between the different people in the organisation who have different skills and responsibilities. AI systems often embody similar modularity: decisions are taken as the outcome of multiple sub-units performing individual calculations whose results are then integrated. One approach to building better AI is to take that idea further: allow vast numbers of different AI modules to discover each other and interact with each other in a decentralised manner, without any predetermined hierarchy. Higher levels of intelligence might emerge from this kind of relationship. That's the driving thought behind, for example, the SingularityNET "AI marketplace"[104].

14: *Provably safe AI*: Most AI development regards safety as a secondary consideration. Yes, software might have bugs, but these bugs can be found and removed later, once they prove troublesome. Yes, software might behave unexpectedly when placed into a new environment – for example, one in which other novel software algorithms have been placed. But, again, these interactions can be reconfigured later, if the need arises. At least, that's the dominant practice behind much of the industry. AI developers might nowadays shy away from the infamous mantra from the early days of Facebook, "Move fast and break things"[105], but they often still seem to be guided by that slogan in practice. However, a minority movement puts the issue of safety at the heart of its research. It's possible that the new designs for AI that arise from this different focus will, as well as being safer, attain new capabilities. These ideas are explored in, for example, the book by Stuart Russell, *Human Compatible: Artificial Intelligence and the Problem of Control*[106].

15: *Combination approaches*: To the fourteen items already on this list, we should add two more that are straightforward: improvements with classical-style AI expert systems, and improvements with deep neural networks. That takes the count to sixteen. Next consider combinations of at least two of these sixteen items: that makes a total of 120 approaches to consider. Adding ideas from a third item into the mix raises the number yet higher (over five thousand). OK, many of these combinations could provide little additional value, but in other cases, who knows in advance what disruptive new insights might arise?

The difficulty of measuring progress

For some tasks, it's relatively easy to predict when a particular target will be reached. That's when the landscape

4. THE QUESTION OF URGENCY

is already well understood, and there are previous examples from which useful comparisons can be drawn.

But when the landscape still contains significant uncertainties, no confident predictions can be made. It's like travelling down a road at a reasonably steady pace, but the road ahead contains a swamp made out of an unknown kind of sticky vegetation. In that case, the vehicle could be held up indefinitely.

In the case of AGI, it's possible to list a number of aspects of human intelligence which it seems no form of AI can currently match. This includes:

1. Being able to learn new concepts from being shown only a small number of examples
2. Having a rich "common sense" that can resolve ambiguities in communications
3. When two data points are correlated, being able to deduce whether one of these points is the cause of the other one.

Different writers include different sets of items in their own versions of this list. It's often the case, however, that forms of AI *can already* deliver the functionality that the writer supposes is beyond AI capability. For example, writing in 2021[107], Kai-Fu Lee, a leading Venture Capitalist, lists "three capabilities where I see AI falling short, and that AI will likely still struggle to master even in 2041":

> ***Creativity.*** AI cannot create, conceptualize, or plan strategically. While AI is great at optimizing for a narrow objective, it is unable to choose its own goals or to think creatively. Nor can AI think across domains or apply common sense.
>
> ***Empathy.*** AI cannot feel or interact with feelings like empathy and compassion. Therefore, AI cannot make

another person feel understood and cared for. Even if AI improves in this area, it will be extremely difficult to get the technology to a place where humans feel comfortable interacting with robots in situations that call for care and empathy, or what we might call "human-touch services."

Dexterity. AI and robotics cannot accomplish complex physical work that requires dexterity or precise hand-eye coordination. AI can't deal with unknown and unstructured spaces, especially ones that it hasn't observed.

As it happens, each item on this list by Kai-Fu Lee can be strongly disputed. AIs are already involved in many creative activities, for example using GANs (as described earlier). AI that includes affective computing can indeed convey feelings of support and empathy to people interacting with that software. And modern robots, using software from Covariant.AI, that are trained in simulated environments before being deployed in the real world, demonstrate remarkable dexterity[108].

In other words, there's scope to disagree with what exactly belongs on the list of tasks that are presently beyond the ability of AI.

Such disagreements shouldn't come as a surprise. They're a consequence of our lack of knowledge of the challenges that still lie ahead. They also reflect our far-from-complete understanding of what is happening inside the human brain. That is, we still only have a rudimentary grasp of the nature of the "general intelligence" which humans possess.

Despite these disagreements, the point is clear that there are at least some aspects of human general intelligence which are currently beyond AI capability. What is *not* clear is:

- How much effort will be required, in order to solve any of these shortcomings
- How independent are the various items on the list.

As a thought experiment, suppose that it were agreed that the list contained seven different items. Suppose also that some AI researchers have a credible idea for a way to improve AI in order to address one of these items. Once that piece of research completes, in line with the idea the researchers had in mind, three outcomes are possible:

1. The research results in a small step forward, but doesn't actually deliver the missing functionality. That missing functionality turns out to be *even harder* to create than expected
2. The research does deliver the expected functionality, *and* it also turns out to deliver *several other items* on the list of seven unsolved problems; in other words, the items weren't as independent as had previously been thought
3. The research delivers just the single piece of missing functionality; six other tasks remain.

It's because all three possibilities are credible, that it's particularly difficult to make any confident predictions about the date by when AGI might emerge.

That realisation should warn us against making either of two forecasting mistakes:

- Wrongly insisting that AGI *cannot* be attained *before* a specified date, such as 2030
- Wrongly insisting that AGI *must surely* be attained *after* a specified date, such as 2065.

Learning from Christopher Columbus

As just reviewed, it's hard to calculate the distance between today's AI and AGI. Accordingly, it's hard to estimate the amount of effort required for a project to convert today's AI into AGI.

This situation can be compared to a problem facing European navigators in the late fifteenth century. They were interested in a particular destination, namely the Far East. In this case, there already was one known route to travel to the destination, namely overland, travelling eastward, following in the footsteps of Marco Polo. But could there be a more convenient route travelling in the opposite direction?

That was the idea of maverick seafarer Christopher Columbus. Columbus spent years trying to drum up support for an idea that most educated people of the time considered to be a hare-brained scheme. These observers believed that Columbus had fallen victim to a significant mistake – he estimated that the distance from the Canary Islands (off the coast of Morocco) to Japan was around 3,700 km, whereas the generally accepted figure was closer to 20,000 km. Indeed, the true size of the sphere of the Earth had been known since the 3rd century BC, due to a calculation by Eratosthenes, based on observations of shadows at different locations.

Accordingly, when Columbus presented his bold proposal to courts around Europe, the learned members of the courts time and again rejected the idea. The effort would be hugely larger than Columbus supposed, they said. It would be a fruitless endeavour.

4. THE QUESTION OF URGENCY

Columbus, an autodidact, wasn't completely crazy. He had done a lot of his own research. However, he was misled by a number of factors[109]:

- Confusion between various ancient units of distance (the "Arabic mile" and the "Roman mile")
- How many degrees of latitude the Eurasian landmass occupied (225 degrees versus 150 degrees)
- A speculative 1474 map, by the Florentine astronomer Toscanelli, which showed a mythical island "Antilla" located to the east of Japan; therefore "the east" might be closer than previously expected.

No wonder Columbus thought his plan might work after all. Nevertheless, the 1490s equivalents of today's VCs kept saying "No" to his pitches. Finally, spurred on by competition with the neighbouring Portuguese (who had, just a few years previously, successfully navigated around the southern tip of Africa[110]), the Spanish king and queen agreed to take the risk of supporting his adventure. After stopping in the Canaries to restock, the Nina, the Pinta, and the Santa Maria set off westward. Five weeks later, the crew spotted land, in what we now call the Bahamas. And the rest is history.

But it wasn't the history expected by Columbus, or by his backers, or by his critics. No-one had foreseen that a huge continent existed in the oceans in between Europe and Japan. No ancient writer – either secular or religious – had spoken of such a continent.

Nevertheless, once Columbus had found it, the history of the world proceeded in a very different direction – including mass deaths from infectious diseases transmitted from the European sailors, genocide and cultural apocalypse, and enormous trade in both goods and slaves. In due course, it would be the ingenuity and initiatives of people subsequently resident in the Americas that propelled humans beyond the Earth's atmosphere all the way to the moon.

Here's the relevance of this analogy to the future of AI.

Rational critics may have ample justification in thinking that true AGI is located many decades in the future. But this fact does not deter a multitude of modern-day AGI explorers from setting out, Columbus-like, in search of some dramatic breakthroughs. And who knows what new *intermediate* forms of AI might be discovered, unexpectedly?

Just as the contemporaries of Columbus erred in presuming they already knew all the large features of the earth's continents (after all: if America really existed, surely God would have written about it in the Bible…), modern-day critics of AGI can err in presuming they already know all the large features of the landscape of possible artificial minds.

When contemplating the space of all possible minds, some humility is in order. We cannot foretell in advance what configurations of intelligence are possible. We don't know what may happen, if separate modules of reasoning are combined in innovative ways.

When critics say that it is unlikely that present-day AI mechanisms will take us all the way to AGI, they are very

4. THE QUESTION OF URGENCY

likely correct. But it would be a serious error to draw the conclusion that meaningful new continents of AI capability are inevitably still the equivalent of 20,000 km into the distance. The fact is, we simply don't know. And for that reason, we should keep an open mind.

One day soon, indeed, we might read news of some new "AUI" having been discovered – some Artificial Unexpected Intelligence, which changes history. It won't be AGI, but it could have all kinds of unexpected consequences.

Of course, every analogy has its drawbacks. Here are three ways in which the discovery of an AUI could be different from the discovery by Columbus of America:

1. In the 1490s, there was only one Christopher Columbus. Nowadays, there are hundreds (perhaps thousands) of schemes underway to try to devise new models of AI. Many of these are proceeding with significant financial backing.
2. Whereas the journey across the Atlantic (and, eventually, the Pacific) could be measured by a single variable (latitude), the journey across the vast multidimensional landscape of artificial minds is much less predictable. That's another reason to avoid dogmatism.
3. Discovering an AUI could drastically transform the future of exploration in the landscape of artificial minds. Assisted by AUI, we might get to AGI much quicker than without it. Indeed, in some scenarios, it might take only a few months after we reach AUI for us (now going much faster than before) to reach AGI. Or days. Or hours.

The possibility of fast take-off

Discussing the possible date for the technological singularity involves two separate questions:

1. How long will it take for AI to match all the thinking capabilities of humans, that is, to reach AGI?
2. How soon after the advent of AGI will AI reach superintelligence – levels of all-round capability that completely surpass human intelligence?

The discussion in this chapter so far can be summarised as follows: there's wide uncertainty about the date at which AGI is reached, but it is unwise to categorically rule out reaching AGI within just a few years' time. That's because any of a number of breakthroughs, that can already be foreseen, could unexpectedly turn out to solve not just one but a number of apparently different problems that have been holding up AGI. And once some extra progress has been made, the additional capabilities created could play important roles in progressing AI yet further.

What remains open for consideration is the second question: once AGI has been reached, how soon thereafter will further improvements take place?

The best answer to this second question is similar to the best answer to the first question: it's not possible to give an answer with any certainty, but it's wise to keep an open mind. That is, it's not possible to rule out the scenario of "fast take-off" in which AGI is able to contribute to the creation of superintelligence within a timescale of perhaps just months or weeks.

4. The question of urgency

The possibility of fast take-off was described in the early 1960s by IJ Good[111], a long-time colleague of Alan Turing:

> Let an ultraintelligent machine be defined as a machine that can far surpass all the intellectual activities of any man however clever. Since the design of machines is one of these intellectual activities, an ultraintelligent machine could design even better machines; there would then unquestionably be an "intelligence explosion," and the intelligence of man would be left far behind. Thus the first ultraintelligent machine is the last invention that man need ever make, provided that the machine is docile enough to tell us how to keep it under control.

In other words, not long after humans manage to create an AGI, the AGI is likely to evolve itself into an artificial superintelligence that far exceeds human powers.

In case the idea seems far-fetched, of an AI redesigning itself without any human involvement, consider a slightly different possibility: humans will still be part of that design process, at least in the initial phases. That's already the case today, when humans use one generation of AI tools to help design a new generation of improved AI tools, before going on to repeat the process.

IJ Good foresaw that too. This is from a lecture he gave at IBM in New York in 1959[112]:

> Once a machine is designed that is good enough..., it can be put to work designing an even better machine...
>
> There will only be a very short transition period between having no very good machine and having a great many exceedingly good ones.

THE SINGULARITY PRINCIPLES

At this point an "explosion" will clearly occur; all the problems of science and technology will be handed over to machines and it will no longer be necessary for people to work. Whether this will lead to a Utopia or to the extermination of the human race will depend on how the problem is handled by the machine.

An AI that is able to reason more precisely and more comprehensively than any human would, in principle, have the following methods to improve its performance yet further:

- Reading and understanding vast swathes of published articles (including many in relatively obscure locations), to notice where important new ideas had been mentioned, which had not yet received an appropriate amount of analysis, regarding their potential to improve AI capability
- Modelling vast numbers of new possibilities in advance, to determine which are likely to result in significant enhancements
- Identifying new ways to connect together different hardware resources, in order to boost the overall computing power available to an AI.

Each time one of these improvements are adopted, it raises the possibility of enabling better research into yet more improvement possibilities.

There's no need to assume the existence of an *indefinite* (unbounded) ongoing sequence of significant improvement steps. All that's necessary is to assume:

- That *some* additional improvements remain possible

- That the reasoning capability of the human brain represents no absolute upper bound on possible general intelligence systems.

On the other hand, other factors could act to slow down these potential improvements. For example, new hardware configurations might require experimentation that takes more time.

But it's by no means obvious, in advance, whether the limiting factor to significant additional improvement will be:

1. A "soft" factor, that can be modified quickly
2. A "hard" factor, whose modification would take longer.

Any presupposition that the second case applies would be reckless.

Therefore, I say again, there is no time to lose.

So without any further preliminaries, let's now review the Singularity Principles themselves.

5. The Principles in depth

The Singularity Principles are a set of recommendations that are intended to increase the likelihood that oncoming disruptive technological changes will have outcomes that are profoundly positive for humanity, rather than deeply detrimental.

The principles split into four areas. The four areas are covered, respectively, in the four following chapters:

1. Methods to analyse the goals and outcomes that may arise from particular technologies;
2. The characteristics that are desirable in technological solutions;
3. Methods to ensure that development takes place responsibly;
4. Evolution and enforcement:
   - How this overall set of recommendations might itself evolve further over time
   - How to increase the likelihood that these recommendations are applied in practice rather than simply being some kind of wishful thinking.

5.1 Analysing goals and potential outcomes

Once projects are started, they can take on a life of their own.

It's similar to the course taken by the monster created by Dr Frankenstein in Mary Shelley's ground-breaking novel. A project – especially one with high prestige – can acquire an intrinsic momentum that will carry it forward regardless of obstacles encountered along the way. The project proceeds because people involved in the project:

- Tell themselves that there's already a commitment to complete the project
- View themselves as being in a winner-takes-all race with competitors
- Feel constrained by a sense of loyalty to the project
- Perceive an obligation to fellow team members, or to bosses, or to others who are assumed to be waiting for the product they are developing
- Fear that their pay will be reduced, and their careers will stall, unless the project is completed
- Desire to ship their product to the world, to show their capabilities.

But the result of this inertia could be outcomes that are, later, bitterly regretted:

- The project produces results significantly different to those initially envisioned
- The project has woeful unexpected side-effects

- Even if it is successful, the project may consume huge amounts of resources that would have been better deployed on other activities.

Accordingly, there's an imperative to *look before you leap* – to analyse ahead of time the goals and potential outcomes we can expect from any particular project. And once such a project is underway, that analysis needs to be repeated on a regular basis, taking into account any new findings that have arisen in the meantime. That's as opposed to applying more funding and other resources regardless.

The bigger the potential *leap*, the greater the need to *look* carefully, beforehand, at where the leap might land.

The Singularity Principles address projects that seek to develop or deploy new technology that might, metaphorically, leap over vast chasms. The first six of these principles act together to improve our collective "look ahead" capability:

- *Question desirability*
- *Clarify externalities*
- *Require peer reviews*
- *Involve multiple perspectives*
- *Analyse the whole system*
- *Anticipate fat tails*

Read on for the details.

Question desirability

The principle of "Question desirability" starts with the recognition that, just because we believe we *could* develop some technology, and even if we feel some *desires* to develop that technology, that's not a *sufficient* reason for us actually to go ahead and develop it and deploy it.

Therefore, the principle urges that we take the time, at the start of the project, to write down what we assume are the good outcomes we will obtain from the technology to be developed. Once these assumptions have been written down, it allows for a more thoughtful and considered review.

The principle also urges that we consider more than one method for achieving these intended outcomes. We should avoid narrowing our choice, too quickly, to a particular technology that has somehow caught our fancy.

This separation in analysis of desired outcomes, sometimes known as "requirements", from possible solutions, is a vital step to avoiding unintended consequences of technologies:

- *Requirements*: The outcomes we desire to obtain, as a result of this project, or possibly from other, different, projects
- *Solutions*: Potential methods of meeting our requirements – though, if we're not careful, we can become preoccupied with achieving a particular solution, and lose sight of key aspects of the underlying requirements.

For example, a requirement could be "reduce the likelihood of extreme weather events". One possible solution is "accelerate the removal of greenhouse gases that have built up in the atmosphere". But a preoccupation with that solution might lead to experimentation with risky geo-engineering projects, and to a failure to investigate other methods to avoid extreme weather events.

5.1 ANALYSING GOALS AND POTENTIAL OUTCOMES

Again, a requirement could be "reduce the threats posed by the spread of weapons of mass destruction". One possible solution is "accelerate the introduction of global surveillance systems". But a preoccupation with *that* solution can have its own drawbacks too.

Once we have documented our requirements, it can make it easier to find better, safer, more reliable ways of achieving the outcomes that we have in mind.

The principle of "Question desirability" also recommends that we should in any case challenge assumptions about which outcomes are desirable, and we should be ready to update these assumptions in the light of improved understanding.

Indeed, we should avoid taking for granted that agreement exists on what will count as a good outcome.

That takes us to the next principle, "Clarify externalities".

Clarify externalities

Recall that an externality is an effect of a project, or the effect of an economic transaction, that is wider than the people directly involved.

Examples of negative externalities include noises, smells, pollution, resource depletion, cultural chaos, and a general loss of resilience. Examples of positive externalities include:

- People learning skills as a result of interacting with each other
- A reduction in the likelihood of non-vaccinated people catching an infection (because the

prevalence of the infection in the population is reduced by the people who *are* vaccinated)
- The free distribution of second-hand books and magazines.

The principle of "Clarify externalities" draws attention to possible wider impacts (both positive and negative) from the use of products and methods, beyond those initially deemed central to their operation. The principle seeks to ensure that these externalities are included in cost/benefit calculations.

Therefore we should not just consider metrics such as profit margin, efficiency, time-to-market, and disabling competitors. We need to consider broader measures of human flourishing.

What makes this analysis *possible* is the effort taken, in line with the "Question desirability" principle, to write down the intended outcomes of the technology to be developed. What makes this analysis *more valuable* are the principles of "Require peer reviews" and "Involve multiple perspectives" to which we turn next.

Require peer reviews

The *alternative* to requiring peer reviews is that we trust the people who are behind a particular project. We may feel they have a good track record in creating technologies and products. Or that they have outstanding talent. In that case, we might feel a peer review would be a waste of time.

That may be acceptable for projects that are sufficiently similar to those undertaken in the past. However, new technologies have a habit of bringing surprises, especially when used in novel combinations.

That's why independent peer reviews should be required, involving external analysts who are not connected with the initial project team. These analysts should ask hard questions about the assumptions made by the project team.

The value of these peer reviews depends on:

- The extent to which reviews are indeed independent, rather than being part of some cosy network of "I'll scratch your back – give your project a favourable review – if you scratch mine"
- The extent to which reviewers have up-to-date relevant understanding of the kinds of things that could go wrong with particular projects.

In turn, this depends upon society as a whole placing sufficient priority on supporting high quality peer reviews.

Involve multiple perspectives

The peer review phase, into the proposed goals and likely outcomes of a project, should involve people with *multiple different skill sets and backgrounds (ethnicities, life histories, etc)*.

These reviewers should include not just designers, scientists, and engineers, but also people with expertise in law, economics, and human factors.

A preoccupation with a single discipline or a single perspective could result in the project review overlooking important risks or opportunities.

To be clear, these independent analysts won't necessarily have a veto over decisions taken by the project team. However, what is required is that the project team, along with their sponsors, take proper account of questions and concerns raised by independent analysts.

That proper account should observe two further principles: "Analyse the whole system" and "Anticipate fat tails".

Analyse the whole system

What's meant by the "whole system" is the full set of things that are connected to the technology that could be developed and deployed – upstream influences, downstream magnifiers, and processes that run in parallel. It also includes human expectations, human beliefs, and human institutions. It includes aspects of the natural environment that might interact with the technology. And, critically, it includes other technological innovations.

When analysing the potential upsides and downsides of using the new technology that we have in our mind, we need to consider possible parallel changes in that wider "whole system".

Some examples:

- Rather than just forecasting that a new intervention in a biological ecosystem might reduce the presence of some predator species with unpleasant characteristics, we need to consider whether a reduction of that population would trigger a sudden rise in the population of another species, preyed on by the first, with knock-on consequences for the flora consumed by the second species, and so on
- Rather than extrapolating the level of public interest in a forthcoming new technology from what appears to be only a modest interest at the present time, we should consider the ways in

which public interest might significantly change – potentially even causing a panic or stampede – once there are visible examples of the technology changing people's lives
- Rather than simply analysing how a piece of new artificial intelligence might behave in the environment as it exists today, we should consider possible complications if other pieces of new artificial intelligence, including adversarial technology, or novel forms of hacking, are introduced into the environment as well.

This kind of analysis might lead to the conclusion that a piece of new technology would, after all, be more dangerous to deploy than was first imagined. Or it could lead to us changing aspects of the design of the new technology, so that it would remain beneficial even if these other alterations in the environment took place.

Anticipate fat tails

The principle of "Anticipate fat tails" urges us to remember that not every statistical distribution follows that of the famous Normal curve, also known as the Gaussian bell curve.

For Normal distributions, once we observe the mean of a set of observations, often denoted by the Greek letter mu (μ), and also the standard deviation of these observations, known as sigma (σ), we can be confident that new measurements more than three standard deviations away from the mean will be unlikely. They'll be seen only around three times in a thousand. And for a new measurement that is more than six standard deviations away from the mean, you would have to wait on average more than one million years, if a new measurement was made every single day[113].

However, our initial observations of the data might lead us astray. The preconditions for the distribution of results being Normal might not apply. These preconditions require that the outcomes are formed from a large number of individual influences which are independent of each other. When, instead, there are connections between these individual influences, the distribution can change to have what are known as "fat tails". In such cases, outcomes can arise more often that are at least six sigma away from the previously observed mean – or even twenty sigma away from it – taking everyone by a horrible surprise.

That possibility would change the analysis from "how might we cope with significant *harm*", such as a result three sigma away from the mean, to "could we cope with total *ruin*", such as a result that is, say, twenty sigma distant.

In practical terms, this means our plans for the future should beware the creation of monocultures that lack sufficient diversity – cultures in which all the variations can move in the same direction at once.

We should also beware the influence of *hidden connections*, such as the shadow links between multiple different financial institutions that precipitated the shock financial collapse in 2008.

For example, consider a cry of exasperation in August 2007 from David Viniar, the Chief Financial Officer for Goldman Sachs[114]. Viniar was offering his explanation for a dismal reversal of fortune in the bank's Global Alpha investment fund. This was no ordinary fund: it used what was described as "sophisticated computer models" to

5.1 ANALYSING GOALS AND POTENTIAL OUTCOMES

identify very small differences in market prices, and to buy or sell securities as a result. The fund had stellar financial results for a number of years, before experiencing a major setback as the global financial crash gathered pace. Viniar's shocked comment: "We were seeing things that were 25-standard deviation moves, *several days in a row*".

Viniar was by no means alone, as a banking executive, at being caught out by the scale of deviations which occurred in the prices of key financial instruments in 2007. John Taylor of Stanford and John Williams of the Federal Reserve Bank of San Francisco have calculated[115] some stunning "before and after" statistics for the so-called "spread" between the overnight interbank lending rate and the London interbank offer rates (Libor). The baseline statistics covered the period from December 2001 to July 2007, that is, the period before the financial crisis. However, the spread on 9th August 2007 exceeded the previous mean by *seven* standard deviations of the baseline statistics. By 20th March 2008, the spread exceeded the previous mean by *sixteen* standard deviations.

The takeaway: the mere fact that performance trends seem to be well behaved for a number of years provides no guarantee against sharp ruinous turns of fortune.

Indeed, whenever there are reasons to foresee fat tail outcomes, it means we need to rethink our plans for the new technology. Otherwise, the world might experience a shock outcome from which there is no prospect of any recovery – perhaps for generations, perhaps indefinitely.

In the next chapter, we'll review the principles covering the characteristics that are highly desired in technological solutions.

5.2 Desirable characteristics of tech solutions

Six of the Singularity Principles promote characteristics that are highly desirable in technological solutions:

- *Reject opacity*
- *Promote resilience*
- *Promote verifiability*
- *Promote auditability*
- *Clarify risks to users*
- *Clarify trade-offs*

Reject opacity

The principle of "Reject opacity" means to be wary of technological solutions whose methods of operation we don't understand.

These solutions are called "opaque", or "black box", because we cannot see into their inner workings in a way that makes it clear how they are able to produce the results that they do.

This is in contrast to solutions that can be called transparent, where the inner workings can be inspected, and where we understand why these solutions are effective.

The principle also means that we should resist scaling up such a solution from an existing system, where any failures could be managed, into a new, larger, system where any such failures could be ruinous.

5.2 Desirable characteristics of tech solutions

As it happens, many useful medicinal compounds have mechanisms that are, or were, poorly understood. One example is the drug aspirin, probably the most widely used medicine in the world after its introduction by the Bayer corporation in 1897. The mechanism of action of aspirin was not understood until 1971[116].

Wikipedia has a category called "Drugs with unknown mechanisms of action"[117] that, as of mid-2022, has 71 pages. This includes the page on "General anaesthetics".

Many artificial intelligence systems trained by deep neural networks have a similar status. It is evident that such an AI often produces good results, in environments that are well defined, but it's not clear *why* it can produce these results. It's also unclear when such an AI system can be misled by so-called adversarial input, or what are the limits of the environments in which that AI will continue to function well.

So long as the overall process is being monitored, and actions can be taken to address failures before these failures become ruinous or catastrophic, opaque systems might, for a while, be an "allowable weakness" with the useful positive side-effect of increasing human wellbeing.

But if there are risks of any failure escalating, beyond the ability of any intervention to fix in a timely manner, that's when these opaque systems need to be rejected.

Instead, more work is needed to make these systems explainable[118] – and to increase our certainty that the explanations provided accurately reflect what is actually happening inside the technology, rather than being a mere fabrication that is unreliable.

Promote resilience

The principle of "Promote resilience" means we should prioritise products and methods that make systems more robust against shocks and surprises.

If an error condition arises, or an extreme situation, a resilient system is one that will take actions to reverse, neutralise, or otherwise handle the error, rather than such an error tipping the system into an unstable or destructive state.

An early example of a resilient design was the so-called centrifugal governor, or flyball governor, which James Watt added to steam engines. When they rotated too quickly, the flyballs acted to open a valve to reduce the pressure again.

Another example is the failsafe mechanism in modern nuclear power generators, which forces a separation of nuclear material in any case of excess temperature, preventing the kind of meltdown which occasionally happened in nuclear power generators with earlier designs.

Following the Covid pandemic and the consequent challenges to supply lines that had been over-optimised for "just-in-time" delivery, there has been a welcome rediscovery of the importance of designing for resilience rather than simply for efficiency. These design principles need to be further elevated. Any plans for new technology should be suspended until a review from a resilience point of view has taken place.

Promote verifiability

The principle of "Promote verifiability" states that we should prioritise products and methods where it is possible

5.2 Desirable characteristics of tech solutions

to ascertain in advance that *the system will behave as specified*, without having bugs in it.

We should also prioritise products and methods where it is possible to ascertain in advance that *there are no significant holes in the specification*, such as failure to consider interactions with elements of the environment, or combination interactions.

In other words, we need increased confidence in each of two steps:

1. The product is specified to behave in various ways, in order that particular agreed goals or requirements will be met in a wide variety of different circumstances (as previously discussed in the section on "Question desirability")
2. In turn, the product is designed and implemented, using various techniques and components, in order that it behaves in all cases in line with the specification.

The principle of "Promote verifiability" urges attention on ways to demonstrate the validity of both of these steps: that the specification meets the requirements, without having dangerous omissions or holes, and that the implementation meets the specification, without having dangerous defects or bugs.

These demonstrations must be more rigorous than someone saying, "well, it seems to work". Different branches of engineering have their own sub-disciplines of verification. The associated methods deserve attention and improvement.

But note that this principle goes beyond saying "verify products before they are developed and deployed". It says that products should be designed and developed *using methods that support thorough and reliable verification*.

Promote auditability

The principle of "Promote auditability" has a similar goal to "Promote verifiability". Whereas "Promote verifiability" operates at a theoretical level, before the product is introduced, "Promote auditability" operates at a continuous and practical level, once the product has been deployed.

The principle urges that it must be possible to monitor the performance of the product in real-time, in such a way that alarms are raised promptly in case of any deviation from expected behaviour.

Systems that cannot be monitored should be rejected.

Systems that can be monitored but where the organisation that owns the system fails to carry out audits, or fails to investigate alarms promptly and objectively, should be subject to legal sanction, in line with the principle "Insist on accountability".

Systems that cannot be audited, or where auditing is substandard, inevitably raise concerns. However, if auditability features are designed into the system in advance, at both the technical level and the social levels, this will help ensure that the technology boosts human flourishing, rather than behaving in abhorrent ways.

Note, again, that this principle goes beyond saying "audit products as they are used". It says that products should be designed and developed *using methods that support thorough and reliable audits*.

Clarify risks to users

The principles that have been covered so far are, to be frank, challenging and difficult.

Compared to these ideals, any given real-world system is likely to fall short in a number of ways. That's unfortunate, and steps should be taken as soon as possible to systematically reduce the shortfall. In the meantime, another principle comes into play. It's the principle of being open to users and potential users of a piece of technology about any known risks or issues with that technology. It's the principle of "Clarify risks to users".

Here, the word "user" includes developers of larger systems that might include the original piece of technology in their own constructions.

The kinds of risks that should be clarified, before a user starts to operate with a piece of technology, include:

- Any potential biases or other limitations in the data sets used to train these systems
- Any latent weaknesses in the algorithms used (including any known potential for the system to reach unsound conclusions in particular circumstances)
- Any potential security vulnerabilities, such as risks of the system being misled by adversarial data, or having its safety measures being edited out or otherwise circumvented.

When this kind of information is shared, it lessens the chances of users of the technology being taken by surprise when it goes wrong in specific circumstances. It will also allow these users to provide necessary safeguards, or to consider alternative solutions instead.

Cases where suppliers of technology fail to clarify known risks are a serious matter, which are addressed by the principle "Insist on accountability". But first, there's one other type of clarification that needs to be made.

Clarify trade-offs

The principle of "Clarify trade-offs" recognises that designs typically involve compromises between different possible ideals. These ideals sometimes cannot all be achieved in a single piece of technology.

For example, different notions of fairness[119], or different notions of equality of opportunity[120], often pose contradictory requirements on an algorithm.

Rather than hiding that design choice, it should be drawn to the attention of users of the technology. These users will, in that case, be able to make better decisions about how to configure or adapt that technology into their own systems.

Another way to say this is that technology should, where appropriate, provide mechanisms rather than policies. The choice of policy can, in that case, be taken at a higher level.

Next, let's review the principles that ensure that development takes place responsibly.

5.3 Ensuring development takes place responsibly

Five of the Singularity Principles cover methods to ensure that development takes place responsibly:

- *Insist on accountability*
- *Penalise disinformation*
- *Design for cooperation*
- *Analyse via simulations*
- *Maintain human oversight*

Insist on accountability

The principle of "Insist on accountability" aims to deter developers from knowingly or recklessly cutting key corners in the way they construct and utilise technology solutions.

A lack of accountability often shows up in one-sided licence terms that accompany software or other technology. These terms avoid any acceptance of responsibility when errors occur and damage arises. If something goes wrong with the technology, these developers effectively shrug their shoulders regarding the mishap. That kind of avoidance needs to stop.

Instead, legal measures should be put in place that incentivise paying attention to, and adopting, methods that are most likely to result in safe, reliable, effective technological solutions.

As always with legal incentives, the effectiveness of these measures will require:

- Regular reviews to check that no workarounds are being used, that allow developers to conform to the letter of the law whilst violating its spirit
- High-calibre people who are well-informed and up-to-date, working on the definition and monitoring of these incentives
- Society providing support to people in these roles of oversight and enforcement, via paying appropriate salaries, providing sufficient training, and protecting legal agents against any vindictive counter suits.

Penalise disinformation

As a special case of insisting on accountability, the principle of "Penalise disinformation" insists that penalties should be applied when people knowingly or recklessly spread wrong information about technological solutions.

Communications that distort or misrepresent features of a product or method should result in sanctions, proportionate to the degree of damage that could ensue.

An example would be if a company notices problems with its products, as a result of an audit, but fails to disclose this information, and instead insists that there is no issue that needs further investigation.

Again, this will require high-calibre people who are well-informed and up-to-date, working on the definition and monitoring of what counts as disinformation. The payment and training of such people is likely to need to be covered from public funds.

Design for cooperation

Another initiative that is likely to need public coordination, rather than arising spontaneously from marketplace interaction, is a strong preference for collaboration on matters of safety. That's in contrast to a headlong competitive rush to release products as quickly as possible, in which short-cuts are taken on quality.

Hence the principle of "Design for cooperation".

For example, public policy could give preferential terms to solutions that share algorithms as open source, without any restriction on other companies using the same algorithms. Related, a careful reconsideration is overdue of the costs and benefits of intellectual property rules.

Public funding and resources should also be provided to support the definition and evolution of open standards, enabling the spirit of "collaborate before competing".

To be clear, the definition and timely evolution of open standards is a hard task. It will (once again) require high-calibre people, who are well-informed and up-to-date, working on the definition and evolution of these standards.

In turn, this is likely to require public subsidy, to ensure that it happens in an effective manner that can win the respect and trust of the companies whose solutions will be impacted.

Analyse via simulations

One factor that has always helped to design and produce new technology is previous technology, including tools and components.

5.3 Ensuring development takes place responsibly

This includes test environments, in which new technology can be put under stress in a variety of circumstances, before being released for wider deployment.

Designing and using test environments in an efficient, effective way is a major engineering discipline in its own right. There's little point in repeating the same test again and again with little variation. That would consume resources and delay product release with little additional benefit. Testing is, therefore, a creative activity. On the other hand, the more that test processes can be automated, the easier it can be to ensure they are completed in a comprehensive manner.

One new factor in recent times is the ability for technology to be tested in virtual environments, that is in simulations. The principle of "Analyse via simulations" urges that attention be given to simulations in which products and methods can be analysed in advance of real-world deployment, with a view to uncovering potential surprise developments that may arise in stress conditions.

Inevitably, each simulation environment is likely to have its own limitations and drawbacks. They won't fully anticipate all the eventualities that may occur in real world situations. However, over time, these simulations can improve, becoming more and more useful, and more and more reliable.

Creating and maintaining best-in-class simulations is likely to require (once again) the support of public funding and resources.

Maintain human oversight

Discussion of the role of simulated environments brings us to the final principle in this section – the principle of "Maintain human oversight".

An increasing role in the development of new technology is being played by automated systems operated via artificial intelligence. These systems assist with the specification, design, implementation, verification, testing, monitoring, and analysis of new technology. They can make the overall process faster and more reliable.

However, although recommendations for next steps in developing products and methods will increasingly originate from software or AI, control needs to remain in human hands. We must ensure that such proposals arising from automated systems are reviewed and approved by an appropriate team of human overseers.

That's because our AI systems are, for the time being, inevitably limited in their general understanding.

It's also the case that any one human is limited in their general understanding. That's why the principles of "Require peer reviews" and "Involve multiple perspectives", covered earlier, come into play. Just as we should avoid putting too much trust into any one AI system, we should avoid putting too much trust into any one human reviewer.

To extend this point: Rather than relying on the analysis of a single AI review system, we should look for ways to have multiple different independent AIs review the recommendations for product development. But in all cases, the final decisions in any contentious or serious matter should pass through human oversight.

This also means that we humans need to regularly practice making independent decisions, without becoming overly dependent on AI tools that might, in unexpected circumstances, mislead us or let us down. Again, simulated virtual environments can provide useful practice situations. A group of humans can take roles in a collaborative "game play", that features the zigs and zags of technology development and deployment in a simulation of competitive, fast-changing circumstances. At the conclusion of the exercise, the participants should conduct a retrospective:

- What did they learn?
- What would they do differently on another occasion?
- What are the limits – and the strengths – of the simulated exercise?

Finally, in this in-depth review of the Singularity Principles, let's move on to the principles covering the evolution and enforcement of the principles themselves.

5.4 Evolution and enforcement

The final area of the Singularity Principles covers how the overall set of recommendations is itself likely to evolve over time, and how the recommendations will be applied in practice rather than simply being some kind of wishful thinking. There are four principles in this area:

- *Build consensus regarding principles*
- *Provide incentives to address omissions*
- *Halt development if principles not upheld*
- *Consolidate progress via legal frameworks*

Since they bridge what could be a yawning gulf between aspiration and actuality, these principles can be seen as the most important in the entire set.

This chapter gives an initial description of these four principles. The remainder of the book explores various questions of practicality and enforcement that arise.

Build consensus regarding principles

The principle of "Build consensus regarding principles" urges that this set of principles be discussed widely, to ensure broad public understanding and buy-in, with conformance in spirit as well as in letter.

In this way, the principles can become viewed as being collectively owned, collectively reviewed, and collectively endorsed, rather than somehow being imposed from outside.

Indeed, society should be ready to update these principles if discussion makes such a need clear – provided the potential change has been carefully reviewed beforehand. There is no assumption of "tablets of stone".

We can be guided in this discussion by applying many of the Singularity Principles, which were initially about the development of technology, to the principles themselves.

This includes the Singularity Principles about goals and outcomes:

- *Question desirability* (of each principle)
- *Clarify externalities* (for each principle)
- *Require peer reviews* (for each principle)
- *Involve multiple perspectives* (for each principle)
- *Analyse the whole system* (for each principle)
- *Anticipate fat tails* (for each principle)

It also includes the Singularity Principles about the characteristics that are desirable in solutions and methods:

- *Reject opacity* (for any of the principles)
- *Promote resilience* (for each principle)
- *Promote verifiability* (for each principle)
- *Promote auditability* (for each principle)
- *Clarify risks to users* (for each principle)
- *Clarify trade-offs* (for each principle)

It's still comparatively early days in this consensus-building discussion.

Provide incentives to address omissions

The principle "Provide incentives to address omissions" states that, where any of this set of principles cannot be carried out adequately, measures should be prioritised to make available additional resources or suitably skilled personnel, so that these gaps can be filled.

This may involve extra training, provision of extra equipment, transfer of personnel between different tasks, altering financial incentive structures, updating legal rules, and so on.

However, if the gap grows too large, between the recommendations of the principles, and prevailing industry practices, something more drastic is needed.

That brings us to the principle of "Halt development if principles are not upheld".

Halt development if principles are not upheld

In case any of these Singularity Principles cannot be carried out adequately, and measures to make amends are blocked, any further development of the technology in question should be halted until such time as the principles can once again be observed.

This may be viewed as a shocking principle, but it was applied very successfully as part of the revolutionary lean manufacturing culture developed in Toyota in Japan from the 1930s onward[121]. Toyota executives realised it was actually to the competitive advantage of their company if each and every employee on their production line was able, on noticing a significant problem with the production, to pull a cord to temporarily halt production of that product. The brake meant that wide attention was quickly brought to bear on whatever quality issue had been noticed. Production throughput slowed down in the short term, but quality throughput and reliability increased in the medium and longer term.

5.4 Evolution and enforcement

But as just noted, adopting this principle means a slowdown in production in the short term, which some companies may consider to put them at a fundamental disadvantage against faster-moving competitors. Moreover, some companies, out of their own bias toward thinking their solutions have very special qualities, may not agree with the appropriateness of some of the principles given earlier. They may wish to rush on regardless. As in the famous phrase that was Facebook's motto for many years, they are prepared to "Move fast and break things", thinking that if things do get broken, they will be easy enough to fix afterward.

That thought – "move fast and break things" – is opposed by an idea expressed at a famous lecture in 1923 at Cambridge University by biologist JBS Haldane, entitled "Daedalus, or Science and the Future"[122]. Haldane reflected on the growing power of science. Observing the progressive increase in these powers, he suggested that these powers are "only fit to be placed in the hands of a being who has learned to control himself". He went on to say, in a phrase that others have subsequently often repeated, that "man armed with science is like a baby armed with a box of matches".

No one likes to be told they are "like a baby", especially if they have a past history of developing remarkable technology. However, from a certain point of view, we all lack sufficient forethought and control to simply "move fast and break things", when what we might break has such explosive potential.

So how do we ensure that production is halted, if necessary, before it reaches an explosive phase? The answer is in the final principle in the entire set.

Consolidate progress via legal frameworks

The principle "Consolidate progress via legal frameworks" states that we should embed aspects of these principles in legal frameworks, to make it more likely that they will be followed.

There needs to be appropriate penalties for violating these frameworks, just as there are already penalties in place when companies violate any of a range of existing regulations on health and safety, or on truthfulness in advertising, or on the presentation of financial information.

These legal frameworks will need to have trenchant backing from society as a whole. After all, some of the companies that are rushing ahead to create more powerful technologies have huge financial motivations to evade legal restrictions. These companies are receiving extensive investments, from banks or venture capitalists, under the assumption that they can produce and maintain a decisive competitive advantage. They are motivated to keep many of their plans under tight reins of secrecy. Via the extensive budgets at their command, they can purchase the support of tame politicians. As such, they form what might appear to be an irresistible force. And as such, they will need to be challenged by an equally strong counterforce.

That counterforce is politics – or, better said, *democratic politics*. History teaches us that governments can, on occasion, build sufficient public support to impose a change of direction on major corporations. For example, anti-trust legislation in the US from the 1890s onward trimmed the power of large conglomerates or cartels in railways, steel, tobacco, oil, and telecommunications, helping to prevent monopoly abuse. Other legislation restricted widespread fraudulent or unsafe practice in fields such as food preparation and the distribution of supposed medicines (which were often "snake oil").

Of course, just as there can be serious anti-social consequences of over-powerful corporations, there can be serious anti-social consequences of over-powerful politicians. Just as there are well-known failure modes of free markets, there are well-known failure modes of political excess. Just as corporations need to remain under the watchful eye of society as a whole, the political framework also needs to be watched carefully by society.

That's why I said that the counterforce to dominant corporations should be, not just politics, but democratic politics – politics that (when it works well) responds quickly to the needs and insights of the entire population.

Moreover, just as the content of the Singularity Principles needs to be subject to revision following public debate, the corresponding legal statutes likewise need to be subject to prompt revision, whenever it becomes clear, following appropriate public review, that they need amending. In other words, the legal frameworks need to combine both strength and adaptability.

None of this will be easy. It will require high calibre politics to ensure it works well. It will also require high calibre *geopolitics*, to ensure a suitable level playing field on the international stage.

Is it credible to look forward to "high calibre politics" and "high calibre geopolitics"? For discussion of these and related questions, let's consider in the next chapter the key success factors for the Singularity Principles.

6. Key success factors

This chapter looks at a number of what can be called "key success factors" for the Singularity Principles, meaning the factors that are likely to have the biggest influence on whether these principles will meet their objectives, or will, instead, turn out to be ineffective.

In some cases, these key success factors can boost *voluntary acceptance* of the principles. In other cases, they can boost *enforced compliance*.

These factors can be listed as:

- Public understanding
- Persistent urgency
- Reliable action against noncompliance
- Public funding
- International support
- A sense of inclusion and collaboration.

Public understanding

Voluntary acceptance occurs when people are sufficiently motivated by a genuine desire to follow the set of recommendations. This desire can be boosted by:

- A vivid awareness of the risk pathways – specific ways in which technology development projects could, despite positive intentions, result in catastrophic outcomes
- A clear understanding of the connections between the various recommendations of the Singularity Principles and the outcomes that are likely to arise

- An appreciation that the restrictions recommended by these principles *will not hinder* the timely development of truly beneficial products – so there is no good reason to oppose these restrictions
- A recognition that *everyone* will be compelled to observe the same restrictions, and cannot gain any meaningful advantage by breaching the rules; therefore, everyone is in the same boat.

The likelihood of voluntary acceptance can be increased by an ongoing programme of public discussion and mutual education. If successful, this programme will lead to more and more people understanding:

- The benefits likely to arise if the Singularity Principles are followed
- The risks arising if these principles are *not* followed.

If successful, this programme will also:

- Dispel the misunderstandings and exaggerations of the Singularity Shadow
- Assist people to overcome the psychological traits that lead to Singularity denialism.

Persistent urgency

Support for adopting and subsequently adhering to the Singularity Principles depends, not just on a better public *understanding* of what's at stake, but also on how the public *feels* about the issues involved.

A judicious combination of fear and wonder can generate and maintain a very useful sense of urgency:

- A persistent fear of the dreadful catastrophes that may occur in the absence of adoption
- A persistent wonder at the possibility to participate in the remarkable world of sustainable superabundance[123] that can be attained through the wise application of the technologies of NBIC and AGI.

Education and discussion about the Singularity Principles needs to keep both the fear and the wonder alive in the public consciousness – preventing these feelings from being submerged under distraction, intimidation, or confusion.

Reliable action against noncompliance

The enforcement aspect of conformance to the Singularity Principles supplements the voluntary aspect. Once people perceive that free-riders can gain no advantage by evading these principles, but will instead be penalised, it will increase their own readiness to comply.

Reliable action against noncompliance includes:

- A "trustable monitoring" system that is able to detect, through pervasive surveillance, any potential violations of the published restrictions
- Strong international cooperation, by a network of different countries that sign up to support the Singularity Principles, to isolate and remove resources from any maverick elements, anywhere in the world, that violate these principles.

Public acceptance of trustable monitoring can accelerate once it is understood that the systems performing the surveillance can, indeed, be trusted; they

6. Key success factors

will not confer any inappropriate advantage on any grouping able to access the data feeds.

Public funding

Many of the Singularity Principles depend upon skilled resources being available to carry out key tasks. In some cases, these resources may be provided by commercial companies. However, to ensure that these resources can take a sufficiently independent stance, they are likely to need to be supported by public funds.

The principles in question include:

- Insist on accountability
- Penalise disinformation
- Design for cooperation
- Analyse via simulations
- Build consensus regarding principles
- Provide incentives to address omissions
- Halt development if principles are not upheld

The funding is necessary to provide:

- Appropriate salaries and other incentives
- Suitable training
- Sufficient support staff, IT systems, and other assistance.

Public support for such funding will depend on:

- The degree to which the public understands the need for such funding (see previous sections)
- Confidence that these funds are being deployed in an effective, unbiased way, free from corruption, self-serving officials, or any excess of bureaucracy.

International support

The same factors that are key to the success of the Singularity Principles in any given country also need to apply on the worldwide arena. Otherwise:

- Companies (or countries) that wish to accept the principles will be concerned about being placed at a competitive disadvantage; their concern is that companies (or countries) that skimp on the application of effort and resources to conform with the principles may build technology that reaches the market more quickly and, at least in the short term, appears to have better performance
- Companies (or countries) that evade the principles may create technology with a catastrophic error mode whose failure would impact, not just their local area, but the entire world.

What is required is the application on the world level of the same factors from individual countries:

- Public discussion and public education, leading to public buy-in, despite ideological or other tensions between different countries
- Monitoring of potential infringements
- Removal of resources from entities that are detected as violating the principles.

Adoption of these practices won't happen at the same speed over the entire world. However, it can start with smaller groups, such as the G7 group of nations, and expand in stages from there.

A sense of inclusion and collaboration

Any set of regulations that is *perceived as being imposed from outside* inevitably raises suspicion and distrust. People will think to themselves that they are being asked to give up some important freedoms, or to do without valuable products and services, mainly for the benefit of apparent "elites" or "outsiders".

Accordingly, the Singularity Principles need to be understood as being in the shared interest of all citizens of all countries on the planet – with no-one left behind against their will. It needs to be understood that the benefits arising from adherence to these principles will reach everyone, and will be dramatic.

Moreover, when people notice what appears to be shortcomings or problems with any of the principles, they should feel a desire to be *part of the solution* to whatever issue they have observed, rather than standing back from the process and expecting it to fail.

In other words, what will make the Singularity Principles stronger and more effective is when people in all walks of life are ready to offer constructive suggestions for refinements and improvements to these principles, in a spirit of positive collaboration.

Indeed, given the scale of the challenges faced, constructive suggestions for refinements will surely be needed.

The final set of chapters of this book look forward to what could be core topics in that envisioned forthcoming collaborative discussion.

7. Questions arising

Reviewers of the Singularity Principles are likely to find a number of questions in their minds. The following chapters suggest at least the beginnings of answers to some of these questions:

- Measuring human flourishing
- Trustable monitoring
- Uplifting politics
- Uplifting education
- To AGI or not AGI?
- Measuring progress toward AGI
- Growing a coalition of the willing

In each case, the points made are part of what is a necessary larger discussion about the feasibility and desirability of various aspects of the Singularity Principles.

7.1 Measuring human flourishing

A number of the Singularity Principles feature assessments of the potential impacts on human flourishing of projects to develop or deploy new technology. These include:

- Question desirability
- Clarify externalities
- Involve multiple perspectives
- Analyse the whole system.

These principles emphasise that *human* flourishing isn't always the same thing as *financial* (or *economic*) flourishing. There should be a lot more to assessing the desirability of a project than calculations of profit margins, efficiency, time-to-market, the accumulation of intellectual property, and the inconveniencing or disabling of competitors.

But beyond such economic and financial assessments, what other factors should be considered? And with what relative priority?

Importantly, the Singularity Principles carry no implication that agreement needs to be reached on a single all-encompassing measurement of human flourishing. That's unrealistic and unnecessary. Different technology projects can be evaluated via appeal to different aspects of overall human flourishing. For example, consideration could be given to the potential impact – positive or negative – of a new product on physical health, emotional resilience, human creativity, social cohesion and collaboration, diversity, autonomy, privacy, longer-term sustainability, or the wellbeing of animals.

The fact that a project has some conflicting assessments, according to different criteria, is no reason, by itself, to require the cancellation or redesign of that project. However, what would be wrong is to attempt to *hide* or *ridicule* some of these assessments. Instead, as per the principles of "Clarify risks to users" and "Clarify trade-offs", these conflicting assessments should be part of the open communication about the project. So let's now think more carefully about trade-offs.

Some example trade-offs

Consider a new use of technology, that allows better automation of a task in manufacturing. As a result, the goods being manufactured can be sold at a lower price point. However, some employees will lose their jobs, since their work tasks can now be performed by robots.

Loss of paid jobs, in this kind of situation, is no reason *by itself* to resist the project to develop and deploy that new piece of technology. However, the likelihood of such an occurrence needs to be emphasised in advance, allowing public discussion of possible consequences[124]. These could include re-skilling personnel, and/or the payment of a "basic income" to people who have lost their employment.

Now consider a second example. In this case, a new infectious disease is spreading quickly, causing lots of deaths. Let's call it Cov-24, by loose analogy to Covid-19. Imagine, also, that two methods could be introduced to restrict the deadliness of this disease:

- Strict controls on freedom of movement: people can only mix with others if they wear tight-fitting face-masks

- A vaccination which, alas, has the unfortunate side-effect that around one person in a thousand who receives the vaccine suffers from sudden heart failure some time in the next few days.

In this second example, general attitudes toward the technological intervention of the vaccine are likely to be considerably more antagonistic than in the earlier example of a technological intervention that increases automation in factories. What underlies this difference of attitude, between the two examples, is the understanding that:

- Humans can still flourish, having lives full of meaning and value, even if they lack paid employment
- Humans can *not* continue to flourish, if they suffer a fatal heart failure as the side effect of taking a vaccine.

A third example: suppose that a political regime is in near despair because of constant criticism and agitation from citizens. The regime observes that the protests are impeding their task of effective governance. Strikes are crippling the economy. To address what it perceives to be a crisis, the regime introduces some carefully calibrated chemicals into the water supply. Result: the population becomes much more docile; they no longer express loud dissatisfaction with government policies. In the absence of strikes, the economy booms.

In this case, two different notions of human flourishing have become opposed:

- Having a stable economy, that produces lots of goods for consumption

- Having independence of thought and freedom of speech.

How are such trade-offs and tensions to be evaluated? Which possible uses of technology should the application of the Singularity Principles seek to block, and which should it seek to particularly encourage?

The choice between two alternatives may appear straightforward in some cases. But in other cases, conflicting instincts can run deep in each of two directions.

Let's look at one possible framework that could help resolve these conflicting assessments: an updated version of the Universal Declaration of Human Rights.

Updating the Universal Declaration of Human Rights

Historically, societies often referred to venerable sets of religious codes to guide them in decisions over potential trade-offs between different aspects of human flourishing. These codes were supplemented by reference to legal precedents – past cases that appeared to feature an issue broadly similar to the one presently under debate.

The problems with such references to religious codes and legal precedents are that:

- New technologies raise possibilities – both opportunities and threats – that are significantly different from those experienced in the past
- Different precedents can be cited, that would lead to opposing conclusions.

That's no reason to turn our backs on studies of previous sets of guidelines. A great deal of collective wisdom is embodied in these guidelines. However, it *is* a reason to work hard at *bringing these guidelines up-to-date*.

The set of recommendations which has probably attracted the most sustained thought, regarding the foundations for human flourishing, is the Universal Declaration of Human Rights[125] (UDHR), as adopted by the United Nations General Assembly in 1948.

I anticipate, therefore, that discussion of the application of the Singularity Principles in different cases will take place in parallel with a project to revise and update the UDHR. That project should take into account:

- The many criticisms and alternative formulations of the UDHR that have been raised[126]
- The possibilities for elevated human flourishing via transhumanist states of being[127] – possibilities that do not feature in the current UDHR text.

Constructing an Index of Human and Social Flourishing

One more strand of parallel activity needs to be accelerated. That's the replacement of GDP (Gross Domestic Product) with something that might be called the IHSF – the index of human and social flourishing.

GDP measures the total financial value of goods and services exchanged in the economy. In contrast, the IHSF should *increase* as the requirements for a good quality of life *reduce in cost*; it should fall when more citizens feel they are being "left behind" against their will, or when other catastrophic "landmines" risk being detonated[128].

As an indication of the problems with GDP, note that GDP *rises* when there is deforestation or overfishing.

7.1 MEASURING HUMAN FLOURISHING

To the extent that reporting on the GDP remains prominent in news broadcasts and in political discussion, it will be no surprise if less attention is paid to the broader foundations of human flourishing. That's a tendency we need to counter. A fuller understanding of all-round human flourishing needs to become one of the centrepieces of public discussion.

For examples of the kinds of information that could usefully be aggregated into the IHSF, refer to the UK National Wellbeing Index[129], as produced by the UK's Office of National Statistics.

An example of an area that will likely generate significant discussion, with competing views that will need to be taken into consideration as the IHSF is constructed, is the set of costs and benefits of various protections granted to intellectual property, namely copyrights and patents. These protections each have arguments in their favour, but the entire set of intellectual property rules has consequences that can hinder human flourishing:

- Drugs that are exceptionally expensive
- More focus on obtaining and defending patents than on actually aiding human flourishing
- The development of new solutions being hindered because of a spaghetti of complex licensing terms.

Similar considerations apply to various ranking systems that emphasise numbers of publications. League tables like these can distort the functioning of academia.

This whole discussion may throw up some big surprises. For example, consider the possibility that we might choose to welcome certain kinds of pervasive surveillance. That point arises in the next chapter.

7.2 Trustable monitoring

Consider the potential spread of technology that could be turned into horrific "weapons of mass destruction" (WMDs).

The dangers from WMDs arise from four factors operating together:

1. The *scientific possibility* for various technologies to be weaponised – creating biological pathogens, nerve gases, nuclear bombs, electromagnetic pulses, and so on
2. The *desire* of a group of alienated individuals to use such a weapon – out of a sense of deep grievance against society, humanity, or their own existence
3. The *ability* of such people to access the materials required to inflict the damage they desire to exert
4. The plans of such people *remaining "under the radar"* – not being noticed by any intelligence services.

Unfortunately, it only requires a very small number of people to be deeply disgruntled with life, and to desire to exert "revenge", for the risk of acquisition and usage of WMDs to be alarming.

Moore's Law of Mad Scientists

This issue was stated in a thought-provoking form by pioneering rationality advocate Eliezer Yudkowsky at the Stanford "Accelerating Change" conference in 2005[130]:

> Moore's Law of Mad Scientists:
>
> The minimum IQ required to destroy the world drops by one point every 18 months.

7.2 Trustable monitoring

The reference, here, is to the original "Moore's Law", which can be stated loosely as "The hardware computing power of silicon chips doubles, for a given price point, every 18 months". The "Mad Scientists" variant highlights the fact that advanced technologies are increasingly easy to find, configure, and deploy.

As Oxford philosopher Nick Bostrom has pointed out, in his 2019 article "The Vulnerable World Hypothesis"[131], it was fortunate that nuclear weapons require considerable sophistication to produce:

> Making an atomic weapon requires several kilograms of plutonium or highly enriched uranium, both of which are very difficult and expensive to produce. However, suppose it had turned out otherwise: that there had been some really easy way to unleash the energy of the atom – say, by sending an electric current through a metal object placed between two sheets of glass.

If it had turned out to be easier to create atomic weapons, it would very likely have increased the chances of them being used more frequently. Fringe groups could have obtained these weapons and detonated them for their own convoluted purposes.

Thankfully, humanity escaped that particular bullet, so to speak. But as science and technology progress, new options for easy access to vastly destructive forces remain a matter of grave concern. New WMDs might not require any fundamental breakthrough; instead, the mere convergence of existing technologies, combined in an unexpected way, could be all that it takes to place terrible explosives within the grasp of people with the adverse psychological disposition to wield them in anger.

Four projects to reduce the dangers of WMDs

In principle, reducing the likelihood of wide use of WMDs involves four projects:

1. Making it clear to as many people as possible that a bright future awaits them, in a future sustainable superabundance, in which case their motivation to initiate mass destruction should diminish
2. Keeping track of the set of possible WMDs which recalcitrant members of society might be able to utilise – noting that this set will grow in size over time, as science and technology evolve
3. Developing counter measures to deploy against potential WMDs
4. Monitoring for signs of any plans to use WMDs.

The last of these projects is, doubtless, controversial. It involves part of society surveilling citizens in ways that could be considered deeply intrusive. Such surveillance could enable state authorities to place undue constraints on members of the public. In other words, if not overseen carefully, *legitimate* surveillance could be accompanied by *illegitimate* surveillance.

The answer is to develop systems of "trustable monitoring".

Detecting mavericks

To be clear, the goal of a system of trustable monitoring goes further than detecting the actions of people who are *intentionally* planning some kind of mass destruction. The system would also have great value in detecting the actions of people who are *risking mass destruction, without intentionally*

7.2 Trustable monitoring

planning it. These are people who violate the safety framework contained in the Singularity Principles.

It's similar to an individual taking a decision to drive a motor vehicle whilst having more than the legally allowed levels of alcohol in their blood. Such drivers may assert their own individual freedom, to drive whenever they wish. But society generally deplores such actions – following activism by groups such as Mothers Against Drunk Driving[132]. Drunk driving risks the death, not only of the driver, but also of third parties who are involved in accidents caused by the person's state of inebriation. Freedoms of action by drivers do not extend to freedoms to drive when in a dangerous condition.

Moreover, society generally approves the role of law enforcement officers in noticing drivers who appear to be drunk, and in using a breathalyser test kit in such circumstances.

A critic might complain that the privacy of an individual driver is violated by the actions of police in stopping their car when it is being driven erratically, requiring them to breathe into some test kit, and then storing the evidence of the result of that test. After all, the driver might not want other people to find out that they were driving in a particular location at a particular time – especially if they were meant to be elsewhere at that time. Nevertheless, these drivers have no absolute right to privacy when they are violating agreed safety rules.

In the same way, organisations that take maverick actions when creating new technology – actions that pose significant risks to the wellbeing of third parties – lose the right to complain about any records made regarding these actions.

Examples of trustable monitoring

The system of trustable monitoring I have in mind will be somewhat similar to the way in which society trusts medical doctors with sensitive medical information. Doctors found to have misused such information – or to have been careless with it – are subject to fines, loss of privileges, or other penalties. Likewise, in a corporation, members of the IT department have privileged access to some of the company's key information stores, and are, again, required to make sparing use of such powers. Again, all commercial aircraft carry cockpit voice recorders, with the recordings being accessed only in case of accident. As one final example, lawyers often see information that is kept out of the public eye.

To avoid abuse, trustable monitoring requires an agreed separation of powers. Each of us might individually dislike the idea that our actions could be monitored, on the off-chance that we are preparing to acquire and deploy WMDs. However, that's a freedom we may agree to give up, as part of *a collective social agreement*, in order to reduce the chance that WMDs are acquired and deployed anywhere within society. The degree to which we are comfortable to accept such a trade-off will depend on the degree to which we can trust the part of society that is doing the monitoring. In turn, that depends on the overall quality of the political infrastructure within our society.

To be clear, there's a significant difference between the kind of trustable monitoring I'm proposing, and the earlier examples of restricted access to private data by doctors, IT technicians, aircraft crash analysts, and lawyers. In these earlier examples, the surveillance has the approval of the people being surveilled. Patients might not want their medical records released to friends or work colleagues, but they acknowledge that their doctors should have sight of that information. However, a would-be mass bomber will take steps to prevent *anyone* from finding out about their plans. Accordingly, to be effective, the monitoring system will presumably need to keep secret some aspects of its methods of gathering information. Critics who have a deep distrust of public officials will be alarmed at any such measures of secrecy. They'll wonder: *what else is being concealed?*

Watching the watchers

The above considerations show why a *separation of powers* is so important.

Any group of "watchers" – units of the state that keep a look out for activities potentially involving WMDs – need to be overseen by a group of "watchers of the watchers" – a separate unit that oversees the operation of the surveillers. Next, the watchers of the watchers will themselves be subject to democratic supervision. Moreover, the entire process is subject to criticism from journalists, analysis by independent researchers, and legal challenges in courtrooms.

As one example, agents of the UK's MI5 security service are subject to review by:

- Internal MI5 supervision
- The Investigatory Powers Commissioner's Office (IPCO)[133]
- The Intelligence and Security Committee (ISC) of Parliament[134].

Public support for these surveillance systems depends on confidence that what is happening behind the scenes is in line with the external description of these systems. Saying one thing but doing something very different under the cloak of secrecy is a recipe for damaging public trust. Any such duplicity could cause "trustable monitoring" to switch, instead, to "contested, despised monitoring". It's all the more reason to insist on the highest standards of integrity in the conduct of such activities.

The people involved in surveillance systems, especially at senior management level, must be beyond suspicion: they should be recognised as carrying out their tasks, not for political or other ulterior purposes, but in line with principles that command bipartisan support.

That implies a higher level of trustworthiness than what is often observed in politics. For fuller discussion about the potential trustworthiness of the political process – and how the assessment of trustworthiness can be transformed by technology – see the next chapter.

7.3 Uplifting politics

One response to several of the recommendations in the Singularity Principles is to fear that "the cure will be worse than the disease".

The worry is that if central authorities take the initiative to write safety rules into legislation, and to fine organisations that violate these rules, this could lead to corruption, to the suppression of vital innovation, and to the entrenchment of regulatory policies that are counter-productive and out-dated.

Indeed, any time that it is proposed that regulations are imposed on fast-changing technological products, critics can object that government regulations will cause worse problems than the ones they are intended to solve. It is said – with considerable justification – that:

- Regulators are frequently out-of-touch with the latest technological possibilities
- Regulators impose delays and inefficiencies on a market, resulting in companies being out-performed by competitors from other countries with looser regulatory systems
- Regulators can be "captured" by vested interests representing today's most dominant companies, to the detriment of smaller, less powerful companies that have more innovative ideas.

These concerns all have merit. But they're no reason to abandon regulations, or to accept the continuation of the risk-laden "anything goes" development culture which, alas, can be found inside many companies.

Instead, these concerns should prompt us *to raise the calibre of our regulatory systems*. Rather than being an out-dated hindrance, these reformed systems will uplift and support development practices that are likely to create truly beneficial products. Rather than being perceived as sluggish bureaucratic swamps, these systems will be widely appreciated for the calibre of the advice provided, and the responsiveness of the personnel who provide the advice.

Such improvements will involve the overcoming of what is, at present, all too often a dysfunctional lack of trust between government departments (as in Washington DC) and the technology companies creating remarkable new products (as in Silicon Valley). These improvements will require better regulators, better politicians, and better relations between these two sets of people.

Uplifting regulators

As just mentioned, better regulations require better regulators. As a matter of priority, we need to take steps so that highly talented people are attracted into the roles of regulator – people with great skills and experience in both technical and legal matters.

Decrying what he observes as a "dangerous... historic divide between Washington and Silicon Valley", distinguished security expert Bruce Schneier offers the following advice[135]:

> We need technologists to get involved in policy, and we need policy-makers to get involved in technology. We need people who are experts in making both technology and technological policy. We need technologists on congressional staffs, inside federal agencies, working for NGOs, and as part of the press. We need to create a

viable career path for public-interest technologists, much as there already is one for public-interest attorneys. We need courses, and degree programs in colleges, for people interested in careers in public-interest technology. We need fellowships in organizations that need these people. We need technology companies to offer sabbaticals for technologists wanting to go down this path. We need an entire ecosystem that supports people bridging the gap between technology and law. We need a viable career path that ensures that even though people in this field won't make as much as they would in a high-tech start-up, they will have viable careers.

In short, we need people working close to politicians – their advisors and staff members – to be more skilled in both the opportunities and risks of regulating technology.

The central role of politics

You may notice a theme emerging:

- *Previous chapter*: The Singularity Principles anticipate better monitoring of what is happening worldwide. But the data collected by that monitoring process could be misused by central authorities. To prevent such misuse, and to build public support for this monitoring, we need to find ways to raise the trustworthiness of the central authorities, and to improve the support environment around these authorities.
- *Present chapter*: The Singularity Principles anticipate better regulations, designed and operated by a group of regulators with higher abilities than many who fill these roles at present. But people with that mix of skills are likely to be disinterested in

7.3 UPLIFTING POLITICS

> working alongside incompetent central authorities. They will run a mile from the stench of political machinations. Therefore, we need to find ways to raise the competence – and character – of people working at the heart of government.

That's a tall order. But I see no real alternative. Happily, as I'll explore in the pages ahead, I see ways in which these improvements can proceed – step by step.

It's as I've said before[136] and will doubtless say again: *The journey to a healthier society inevitably involves politics.*

That's a message many technologists and entrepreneurs are unwilling to hear. They would prefer to ignore politics. They wish, instead, to keep their focus on creating remarkable new technology or on building vibrant new business. Politics is messy and ugly, they say. It's raucous and uncouth. It's unproductive. Some would even say (though I disagree) that politics is unnecessary.

But putting our heads in the sand about politics is a gamble fraught with danger. Looking the other way won't prevent our necks from being severed when the axe falls.

On their present trajectory, technology and business are arguably making politics worse, rather than better. Together, without intending it, they are fuelling increasing dysfunction within politics. In such a setting, technological innovations and aggressive business corporations might end up harming humanity much more than they help us.

Numerous examples could be given of flawed politics leading to strings of bad outcomes. These examples would feature perverse economic incentives, vested interests that hold disproportionate power, self-perpetuating industrial complexes, spiralling arms races, regulatory institutions that are caught in lethargy and inertia, and much more. These outcomes, exacerbated by ever-more powerful technology put to sinister use, threaten in turn a hurricane of adverse consequences. Accordingly, fixing politics is one of the central challenges of our time.

However, in the same way that naïve use of technology can make politics worse, wise use of technology can make politics better.

Three types of improvement are possible:

1. Individual politicians can become more responsive and more knowledgeable regarding the opportunities and risks posed by fast-changing technology
2. New political parties (or alliances) can emerge, with the opportunities and risks of technology being central issues for these parties or alliances, rather than matters of occasional, peripheral concern
3. The entire arena of political debate can be reinvigorated: twenty-first century technology can facilitate political debate that is better informed, more engaged, more productive, and genuinely beneficial, via (in the words of Thomas Malone from MIT[137]) "the surprising power of people and computers thinking together".

In this envisioned possible new politics of the near future, decisions can take place informed by the best insight of the population as a whole, rather than being subverted by partisan vested interests. Viewpoints and information that deserve more attention will rise to the top of political discussion, untarnished, rather than being pushed aside or deviously distorted by those who find

7.3 Uplifting politics

them inconvenient. Political discourse will become authentic, rather than contrived. Our politics will become animated by the spirit of constructive curiosity and open collaboration.

Some critics may view that vision as being a fantasy. However, here's how it could gradually come into reality.

Toward superdemocracy

Here's a short statement from the Gettysburg Address made in 1863 by Abraham Lincoln, which has become a short-hand summary of the ideals of democracy:

> Government of the people, by the people, for the people.

Since 1863, society has become considerably more complicated, and governments have taken on additional new responsibilities. In parallel, social institutions have evolved in many ways, and technology has provided numerous new tools that can assist the task of governance. Despite these changes, Lincoln's aspirational statement remains valid. However, these changes mean that the statement deserves to be *extended*.

Various adaptations of the original statement have been suggested. Some of these adaptations recommend a *reduction* in the powers of politicians:

> As little government as possible

Or a variant:

> Politicians with as little power as possible

Such variants are preoccupied with limiting the harm that politicians can do, rather than supporting politicians in the good work they can also do.

Sadly, if politicians have less power, it will allow other groupings to exert themselves more forcefully in society. In the absence of an effective government, people throughout society will be vulnerable to the abuse of power by large corporations, crime syndicates, mafia-style gangs, guerrilla networks, and external armies from neighbouring states.

Instead, here's a better revision of Lincoln's statement:

Government of the people, resources, institutions, and technology,

by the people, institutions, and technology,

for the people, and for consciousness in general.

In this form, the statement summarises a notion I call "superdemocracy"[138].

Superdemocracy will feature better use of both institutions and technology to raise the calibre of politics. It will provide the environment in which the general public can trust their politicians more fully than at present.

Technology improving politics

To give more details, here are ten ways to take advantage of new technology, including tools with elements of AI, to support new political mechanisms and institutions:

1. *Real-time fact checking*, which could highlight almost immediately whether there is evidence to contradict (or verify) a claim being made by a politician or their supporters
2. *Real-time logic checking*, that could highlight any invalid jumps in reasoning – or conversely, confirm the soundness of an argument

7.3 Uplifting politics

3. *Real-time source checking*, to verify whether a quotation, image, or video extract may have been altered before being presented, changing its meaning or any implications arising
4. *Reputation systems*, that keep track of the reliability of people's past contributions to particular topics
5. *The creative generation of new proposals*, that can combine key elements from previous suggestions in ways that address earlier concerns
6. *Simulations*, in huge computational models, of potential consequences of envisioned legislative changes, to help the identification and evaluation, ahead of time, of possible real-world risks and benefits of these changes
7. *Improved electoral systems*, involving elements of proportional representation as well as ranked preference votes, to avoid the present situation in which far too many people feel that their votes will be essentially meaningless, or that they ought to cast a tactical vote for a candidate different from their actual first preference
8. *Liquid voting*, in which citizens can temporarily assign their voting rights in specified topic areas to people they trust to vote on their behalf regarding these topics
9. *Facilitated citizens' assemblies*, that act in similar ways to jury trials, with representative groups of citizens being selected at random, and supported in a task to evaluate possible solutions to given social issues, ahead of the conclusions of these assemblies being forwarded to society as a whole for wider consideration

10. *A "House of AI" revising chamber of government*, that applies AI reasoning to provide feedback on proposed legislation, as well as offering possible revisions to that legislation.

Transcending party politics

Although temptations to minimise *politics itself* should be resisted, there are strong arguments to minimise *party politics*. It's the partisan aspects of politics that cause most problems, and which need to be diminished.

Political parties made sense in previous times, but nowadays are more of an impediment than an aid to effective government. Political parties multiply mistrust: people in different parties profoundly mistrust each other.

In the past, political parties provided the support for people interested in becoming involved in politics, including training, networks of potential connections, financial assistance, and help with the key task of becoming elected. In turn, politicians were expected to show loyalty to their parties, such as:

1. Voting for policies chosen by party leaders, regardless of their own personal assessments of these policies
2. Joining with party colleagues to pour scorn on opposing parties.

It's true that thoughtful disagreement is a necessary part of life, especially when circumstances are complex. To help clarify the strengths and weaknesses of different ideas, groups of people can usefully take on the task of debate, exploring and advocating different positions. Such disagreement features regularly in science, and science is

7.3 Uplifting politics

the better for it. It's the same with politics. However, *party* politics damages the nature of these debates:

1. Rather than focusing on which *policy* is best, the debate often becomes, in effect, which *party* is best – with attention drawn to purported errors made in the past by various parties, even if these errors have little direct relevance to the current policy debate
2. Disagreements are often magnified, for theatrical purposes, rather than compromises being sought
3. Even when politicians are aware of particular pluses or minuses of a given policy, they often keep silent about these points, since they would run counter to their party's official position
4. When politicians perceive that a point someone is making is damaging to their cause, they often attempt to suppress that voice, or to misrepresent or ridicule it, or to damage the reputation of the people involved – rather than engaging honestly with the substance of the point.

When circumstances are *particularly* complex, with fast-changing possibilities – as in the present day, with the consequences of NBIC technologies becoming ever more prominent – it's especially important to rescue political dialogue from the rancour and distortions of partisanship. The drawbacks of entrenched partisan politics may have been a tolerable weakness in past decades, but are nowadays becoming ever more perilous. It's time, therefore, for the dominance of parties to recede.

Happily, many of the forms of support for prospective politicians, which used to be available only from political parties, are nowadays available from non-party sources, including online networks, and non-partisan think tanks.

In this vision, there will still be a role for political parties to fulfil, but these parties will be more fluid than before. It will become much more common for:

- People who are associated with one party, to nonetheless support a different party on one or more specific policy areas
- People to move between parties
- New parties to form
- Parties to split and merge, creating new groupings
- Governments to include people from multiple different parties.

The prospects for political progress

Countries around the word vary in the extent to which they are already entering the era of post-partisan politics. Factors which aid that kind of politics include:

1. Voting systems, such as proportional representation, that make it easier for new parties to enter parliament, rather than being squeezed out by electors' fears that any votes for new parties will be "wasted"
2. A tradition of parties forming coalitions, with a clear understanding of the best practice in such relationships
3. A tradition of coalitions working in partnership with individuals from other parties that remain formally outside the coalition
4. Public dissatisfaction with any media that is highly partisan

7.3 Uplifting politics

5. A growing general recognition of the drawbacks of "groupthink" – of which partisan politics is an evident troubling example
6. A reduction in the importance of large financial funding for political parties – due to limits being imposed on political expenditure, and due to the rise of less expensive ways for politicians to spread their messages.

In countries like the US and the UK with a particularly strong tradition of unpleasant partisan politics, including the dominance of first-past-the-post elections, the following developments should provide extra pressure to overcome existing inertia and to experiment with post-partisan politics:

1. Growing comfort level with the kinds of technological assistance that support more sophisticated voting methods
2. Evident successes of post-partisan politics in other countries
3. Evident successes of post-partisan politics at local, state, or regional levels
4. Evident successes of citizens' assemblies, convened to address tough issues, but with their members (hopefully) able to transcend the blinkers of their initial political affiliations as the assemblies proceed.

All these initiatives will progress more smoothly if suitable education is available for students of all ages. That's the subject of the next chapter.

7.4 Uplifting education

When first encountered, some aspects of the Singularity Principles may appear strange, excessive, or even otherworldly:

- The envisioned rapid increase in society's pace of change
- The potential of new technology to inflict catastrophic damage worldwide
- The potential of new technology to enormously improve the human condition
- The urgency of transforming the systems under which new technology is developed and deployed
- The possibility for powerful technology companies to be constructively constrained by politicians and regulators
- The possibility for a system of regulations to be kept updated and relevant
- The possibility for regulators and politicians to meaningfully assist the task of steering the development and deployment of new technology, rather than being a hindrance
- The possibility for politicians in different countries to collaborate in support of the Singularity Principles, despite deep ideological differences between these politicians.

The preceding chapters of this book have provided a number of arguments in support of these possibilities. However, whilst these arguments make good sense from an intellectual point of view, they are likely to strike at least some reviewers as being counter-intuitive.

These feelings of puzzlement arise from lack of familiarity with key material that should be part of everyone's education. Accordingly, full buy-in for the Singularity Principles will depend on public actions to remedy these shortcomings in the education syllabus.

That brings us to the *Vital Syllabus* project[139]. This project aims to gather together excellent resources to boost educational possibilities worldwide. It explicitly addresses this question:

> In our age of multiple pressures, dizzying opportunities, daunting risks, and accelerating disruption, what are the most important skills and principles to cherish and uphold?

The project highlights resources that can best assist students of all ages:

- To acquire and deepen these skills
- And to understand and embody the associated principles.

The criteria for resources to be included in the project are that these resources should be:

- *Accessible*: available without any payment or other obstacle
- *Clear*: easy to understand
- *Engaging*: inspiring and keeping the attention of viewers
- *Focused*: addressing the topic in the syllabus, rather than lots of other questions
- *Authoritative*: having good reason to be trusted.

Top level areas of the Vital Syllabus

The structure of the Vital Syllabus materials is subject to revision. At the present time, the materials are structured into twenty-four top level areas, as follows:

1. *Learning how to learn*: How to pick up new skills quickly and reliably
2. *Communications*: Communications with a variety of different kinds of audiences
3. *Agility*: How to manage uncertainty
4. *Creativity*: Going beyond existing methods and solutions
5. *Augmentation*: Technology and tools to boost abilities
6. *Collaboration*: Becoming wiser and stronger together
7. *Emotional health*: Nurturing emotional strength
8. *Physical health*: Factors impacting physical health
9. *Foresight*: Anticipating the unexpected
10. *Leading change*: Inspiring and maintaining transformations
11. *Technologies*: In history, the present, and the future
12. *Economics*: In history, the present, and the future
13. *Governance*: In history, the present, and the future
14. *Democracy*: In history, the present, and the future
15. *Geopolitics*: Influencing political processes, nationally and internationally
16. *Numeracy*: Arithmetic and analysis for the modern age
17. *Science*: Distinguishing "good science" from "bad science"
18. *Philosophy*: Thinking about thinking
19. *Transhumanism*: A philosophy particularly suited to the 2020s
20. *Culture*: The basis for extended flourishing
21. *The environment*: The context in which humanity exists

22. *Landmines*: Identifying and addressing the biggest risks ahead
23. *The Singularity*: Options for the advent of artificial superintelligence
24. *Ultimate futures*: Beyond the event horizon

Improving the Vital Syllabus

The Vital Syllabus project welcomes assistance from anyone who shares the goals of the project. For more details, see the FAQ page for the project[140].

7.5 To AGI or not AGI?

As we approach the conclusion of this review of the Singularity Principles, this question demands an answer:

Should all *attempts to move beyond narrow AI systems to AGI be resisted?*

After all, despite the many good ideas in the Singularity Principles, there is no guarantee that these ideas will prove successful.

Despite our best endeavours:

- AGI might emerge with a set of fundamental values that are misaligned with human flourishing
- AGI is likely to withstand any attempts by humans to control it.

The question "To AGI or not AGI?" splits into three:

1. The *feasibility* of coordinating worldwide action
2. The *desirability* of preventing the creation of AGI
3. The *clarity* of a dividing line between AI and AGI.

Global action against the creation of AGI?

Any attempts to prevent the creation of AGI would need to apply worldwide. Otherwise, whilst *some* countries might abstain from AGI, *other countries* could proceed with projects that, intentionally or otherwise, give rise to AGI.

Is such a system of worldwide control conceivable?

The Singularity Principles themselves conceive of such a system:

- Adherence to a set of principles will initially be agreed in a subset of countries

7.5 To AGI or not AGI?

- Countries outside the agreement will be subject to economic sanctions and other restrictions, in the event that technology projects inside these countries fail to comply
- The set of countries that accept the principles will eventually extend to the entire world.

However, the Singularity Principles don't require the prevention of the creation of AGI. They only require the acceptance of framework conditions, which are designed to increase the likelihood of AGI being profoundly beneficial for humanity.

Compared to any blanket ban, such framework conditions would be easier for countries to accept. That framework doesn't rule out the creation of AGI. It just rules out various dangerous developmental shortcuts.

However, if there is indeed an argument that, despite all the recommendations and regulations of the Singularity Principles, AGI remains too risky, then such an argument could be shared worldwide. Such an argument may have the potential to transcend different political ideologies, economic systems, and national perspectives.

Accordingly, it appears to be *credible* that the world might collectively commit not to create AGI. But that presupposes that a sufficiently compelling argument is raised in support of the *desirability* of that outcome.

Does such an argument exist, and does it stack up?

Possible alternatives to AGI?

The reasons, on the contrary, *to want to create* AGI can be summarised as follows:

1. Sheer curiosity: is AGI something that is actually possible?
2. A desire to learn more about human minds by comparison with whatever kind of mind an AGI possesses
3. A desire to take advantage of the additional intelligence of an AGI to solve problems that are currently beyond human capability.

The third of these reasons matches what DeepMind founder Demis Hassabis has said[141] on a number of occasions to be the purpose of his company's work with AI:

> Solve intelligence, and then use that to solve everything else...
>
> Cancer, climate change, energy, genomics, macroeconomics, financial systems, physics: many of the systems we would like to master are getting so complex. There's such an information overload that it's becoming difficult for even the smartest humans to master it in their lifetimes. How do we sift through this deluge of data to find the right insights? One way of thinking of AGI is as a process that will automatically convert unstructured information into actionable knowledge. What we're working on is potentially a meta-solution to any problem.

Any decision to *prevent* the creation of AGI will need to reconcile with abandoning these specific aspirations. For many people, that will be a deeply unpopular decision. They will say that AGI represents humanity's best hope for solving problems such as the ones Hassabis lists.

Here's what could make that decision more palatable: the belief that solutions to these problems could be

7.5 TO AGI OR NOT AGI?

attained using lesser technological innovations, such as nanotechnology and narrow AI.

We don't yet know whether these lesser technologies will be sufficient to solve cancer, climate change, and so on. But that possibility might become clearer in the years ahead.

In such a case, the world might decide as follows:

- Allow constrained, limited investigations of AI, and into other technologies
- Prevent any developments that could allow AGI to emerge.

A dividing line between AI and AGI?

However, a decision like the one just suggested would face profound practical difficulties. It's not just the question of coordinating global enforcement, addressed earlier in this chapter. It's also the question of knowing which developments "could allow AGI to emerge".

The crux of the uncertainty here is our lack of agreement on which existing trends in AI development might lead, unexpectedly, to the kind of general AI which introduces new problems of alignment and control.

For example, consider the question as to whether scaling up existing methods of deep reinforcement learning will be sufficient to reach AGI. Four researchers from DeepMind submitted an article in June 2021 to the peer reviewed journal *Artificial Intelligence* entitled "Reward is enough"[142]. Here's the abstract:

> In this article we hypothesise that intelligence, and its associated abilities, can be understood as subserving the maximisation of reward. Accordingly, reward is enough

to drive behaviour that exhibits abilities studied in natural and artificial intelligence, including knowledge, learning, perception, social intelligence, language, generalisation and imitation. This is in contrast to the view that specialised problem formulations are needed for each ability, based on other signals or objectives. Furthermore, we suggest that agents that learn through trial and error experience to maximise reward could learn behaviour that exhibits most if not all of these abilities, and therefore that powerful reinforcement learning agents could constitute a solution to artificial general intelligence.

That article represents a minority view within the community of AI researchers. However, it seems rash to completely rule out the hypothesis that it makes. As the renowned blogger Scott Alexander has recently argued in an article in Astral Codex Ten[143], it's by no means inconceivable that increased "AI size" will "solve [all the] flubs [mistakes]" of present-day AI systems.

If humanity wishes to remain in safety, it would therefore need to restrict attempts to scale up existing deep learning reinforcements systems. Again, this policy would bring its own problems, since it's unclear which types of modifications to existing systems might be sufficient to raise the *effective* scale of an AI system and thereby tip it over the threshold into AGI.

It's the same with almost every other current project to improve aspects of today's AI. There's always a risk that such improvements would bring AGI closer. Could *all* these projects be halted? That seems extremely unlikely.

7.5 TO AGI OR NOT AGI?

A practical proposal

Given the severe difficulties facing any attempt at a blanket ban on research that could lead to AGI, the following approach appears more likely to win wider support:

- Mandate that the effort and resources placed into improving the capabilities of AI should be matched by effort and resources placed into improving the safety and beneficence of AI.

Rather than trying to slow down the creation of AGI, this proposal urges a dramatic speed up of work on the methods to steer AGI in positive directions.

For example, research needs to be mandated into:

- Methods to boost alignment and/or control that would be applicable to any powerful AI system
- The most effective ways to raise public awareness and understanding of the risks and opportunities of AGI
- The most useful ways to involve politicians and legislators in these discussions
- How to identify in advance likely thresholds between narrow AI and AGI
- How to detect, reliably, when an AI system is approaching any such threshold – before such a transition becomes unstoppable
- How to be able to pivot sharply in any case when an AI system is approaching the AGI threshold.

The question of how to measure progress toward AGI is the subject of the next chapter.

7.6 Measuring progress toward AGI

Estimates of progress toward the creation of AGI have a colourful history.

It's easy to find past examples when AGI was predicted to happen within a short space of time.

For example, two pioneering AI researchers, Herbert Simon and Allen Newell, made the following predictions at a conference in Pittsburgh in November 1957[144] for events that would happen "within the next ten years" (that is, by 1967):

1. A digital computer will be the world's chess champion

2. A digital computer will discover and prove an important new mathematical theorem

3. A digital computer will write music that will be accepted by critics as possessing considerable aesthetic value

4. Most theories in psychology will take the form of computer programs, or qualitative statements about the characteristics of computer programs

From the vantage point of the 2020s, the timescale elements of these predictions appear ridiculous. That's despite the fact that both Simon and Newell had distinguished academic careers. The two shared the Turing Award in 1975[145], bestowed by the Association of Computing Machinery (ACM) for "contributions to artificial intelligence, the psychology of human cognition, and list processing", and Simon went on to win the Nobel

7.6 MEASURING PROGRESS TOWARD AGI

Prize for Economics in 1978[146]. Evidently, neither of these awards guarantees the soundness of your predictions about the future.

It's also easy to find past examples when apparent experts were sure various landmark accomplishments would *not* take place within a foreseeable future timescale, but AI progress nevertheless did reach these levels.

For example, consider a survey published in May 2014 by Wired journalist Alan Levinovitz[147] of expert opinions about when computers would be able to outperform the best humans at the game of Go. The different experts broadly split into three groups. AI researchers tended to think the task would take "maybe ten years". Professional Go players were more sceptical: the full depths of Go gameplay would more likely resist AI mastery for around twenty years. A third group suggested the task would forever exceed the ability of any mechanical brain – that some kind of "wall" was about to be reached, defying further progress.

However, any simple projection of previous trends was to prove misleading. A significant new disruption arrived, namely the programming methods utilised by Google's London-based DeepMind subsidiary. Rather than needing to wait ten or even twenty years, the breakthrough took less than two years, culminating in an emphatic 4-1 victory by the AlphaGo software over human Go playing legend Lee Sedol in Seoul, South Korea[148]. All the apparent domain experts surveyed by Levinovitz just two years earlier proved to be over-pessimistic by a factor of at least five.

I have heard that some of these forecasters subsequently remarked they never expected that any one organisation would apply to this problem the vast scale of resources that Google chose to deploy. Such a possibility lay outside of what was presumed to be the landscape of plausible scenarios. That misperception is a reminder to all of us to appreciate the potential multiplicative effect of changed human outlook. As in a time of war, or any other major crisis, coordinated human activity can produce results that transcend previous expectations.

Aggregating expert opinions

A number of organisations run projects to aggregate expert forecasts on possible future occurrences. In the systems used by these organisations, greater weight is placed on the forecasts from contributors who have gained good reputation scores following their previous forecasts, and through community ratings of the quality of the explanations they offer in justification of their forecasts.

Consider the organisation Metaculus[149]. One of the founders of Metaculus, the physicist Anthony Aguirre, described the rationale for the site as follows[150]:

> Take the probability that the US will become engaged in a nuclear war. It's (we hope!!) quite small. But how small? There are many routes by which a nuclear war might happen, and we'd need to identify each route, break each route into components, and then assign probabilities to each of these components...
>
> Each of these component questions is much easier to address, and together can indicate a reasonably well-calibrated probability for one path toward nuclear conflict. This is not, however, something we can generally do 'on the fly' without significant thought and analysis.

7.6 MEASURING PROGRESS TOWARD AGI

> What if we do put the time and energy into assessing these sequences of possibilities? Assigning probabilities to these chains of mutually exclusive possibilities would create a probability map of a tiny portion of the landscape of possible futures. Somewhat like ancient maps, this map must be highly imperfect, with significant inaccuracies, unwarranted assumptions, and large swathes of unknown territory. But a flawed map is much better than no map!

Aguirre then set out what would be involved in creating a probability map for forecasts of the sort he envisaged:

> First, it would take a lot of people combining their knowledge and expertise. The world – and the set of issues at hand – is a very complex system, and even enumerating the possibilities, let alone assigning likelihoods to them, is a large task. Fortunately, there are good precedents for crowdsourced efforts: Wikipedia, Quora, Reddit, and other efforts have created enormously valuable knowledge bases using the aggregation of large numbers of contributions.
>
> Second, it would take a way of identifying which people are *really really* good at making predictions. Many people are terrible at it – but finding those who excel at predicting, and aggregating their predictions, might lead to quite accurate ones. Here also, there is very encouraging precedent. The Aggregative Contingent Estimation[151] project run by IARPA, one component of which is the Good Judgement Project[152], has created a wealth of data indicating that (a) prediction is a trainable, identifiable, persistent skill, and (b) by combining predictions, well-calibrated probabilities can be generated for even complex geopolitical events.

Finally, we'd need a system to collect, optimally combine, calibrate, and interpret all of the data. This was the genesis of the idea for Metaculus...

Since the public launch of Metaculus in 2015, the project has attracted a significant community of dedicated forecasters, and it regularly publishes updates on the collective performance of the site[153].

Metaculus predictions

Metaculus has a number of questions regarding the timing of the advent of AGI.

One such question is "Date Weakly General AI is Publicly Known"[154], with the following definition:

- *Able to reliably pass a Turing test of the type that would win the Loebner Silver Prize[155].*
- *Able to score 90% or more on a robust version of the Winograd Schema Challenge[156], e.g. the "Winogrande" challenge[157] or comparable data set for which human performance is at 90+%*
- *Be able to score 75th percentile (as compared to the corresponding year's human students; this was a score of 600 in 2016) on all the full mathematics section of a circa-2015-2020 standard SAT exam, using just images of the exam pages and having less than ten SAT exams as part of the training data. (Training on other corpuses of math problems is fair game as long as they are arguably distinct from SAT exams.)*
- *Be able to learn the classic Atari game "Montezuma's revenge" (based on just visual inputs and standard controls) and explore all 24 rooms based on the equivalent of less than 100 hours of real-time play.*

As of June 2022, a total of 497 forecasters had submitted a total of 1,540 predictions of that date. The community average prediction is October 2028.

Another Metaculus question sets a more demanding definition of AGI: "Date of Artificial General Intelligence"[158]. The criteria for this prediction are:

- *Able to reliably pass a 2-hour, adversarial Turing test during which the participants can send text, images, and audio files (as is done in ordinary text messaging applications) during the course of their conversation. An 'adversarial' Turing test is one in which the human judges are instructed to ask interesting and difficult questions, designed to advantage human participants, and to successfully unmask the computer as an impostor. A single demonstration of an AI passing such a Turing test, or one that is sufficiently similar, will be sufficient for this condition, so long as the test is well-designed to the estimation of Metaculus Admins.*

- *Has general robotic capabilities, of the type able to autonomously, when equipped with appropriate actuators and when given human-readable instructions, satisfactorily assemble a (or the equivalent of a) circa-2021 Ferrari 312 T4 1:8 scale automobile model[159]. A single demonstration of this ability, or a sufficiently similar demonstration, will be considered sufficient.*

- *High competency at diverse fields of expertise, as measured by achieving at least 75% accuracy in every task and 90% mean accuracy across all tasks in the Q&A dataset developed by Dan Hendrycks et al[160].*

- *Able to get top-1 strict accuracy of at least 90.0% on interview-level problems found in the APPS benchmark introduced by Dan Hendrycks, Steven Basart et al[161].*

> *Top-1 accuracy is distinguished, as in the paper, from top-k accuracy in which k outputs from the model are generated, and the best output is selected.*

Again as of June 2022, a total of 239 forecasters had submitted a total of 581 predictions of this date. The community average prediction in this case is April 2038.

Neither of these two dates – 2028 or 2038 – should be regarded as somehow fixed or exemplary. Indeed, these two dates regularly change, as the community of Metaculus forecasters continues to take stock of the latest news and theories about AI performance.

The particular value of these forecasts comes from paying attention to significant changes in the dates predicted.

By the way, in case you're shaking your head in disbelief at the prospect of AGI arriving as early (in various formats) as 2038 or even 2028 – in case you suspect the Metaculus community is dominated by crazed fantasists – here's something to consider. It's a brief list of examples of how a single conceptual breakthrough transformed an entire field of study, leading to progress much faster than the previous trend would have predicted:

- Once physicists Werner Heisenberg and Erwin Schrodinger had established the basics of quantum mechanics in 1925 and 1926, a flood of new results came thick and fast in the next few years. Another pioneer of that subject, Paul Dirac, later referred to this period as a "golden age in theoretical physics"[162]: "For a few years after that it was easy for any second rate student to do first rate work."

7.6 Measuring progress toward AGI

- Earlier, the invention of calculus by Isaac Newton and Gottfried Leibniz, and the formulation of Newton's second law of motion ("F=ma"), had transformed the pace of progress in numerous areas of physics
- In biology, a similar status is held by the principle of evolution via natural selection – although it took considerable time from the original formulation of that principle by Charles Darwin before its full explanatory significance was widely understood. Prominent geneticist Theodosius Dobzhansky put it like this in an essay in 1973[163]: "Nothing in biology makes sense except in the light of evolution."
- Once inventor James Watt had created steam engines that operated with sufficient efficiency, these engines were soon at work not only in coalmines (where they had originated, as a means to pump out water) but also in tin mines and copper mines; they were, moreover, soon revolutionising the operation of mills producing flour, cotton, paper, and iron, as well as distilleries that produced alcohol; not long after that, steam engines gained a further lease of life once they were built into railway locomotives and paddle ships
- The breakthrough success in computer vision in 2012 of the "AlexNet" convolutional neural network, designed by Alex Krizhevsky with support from Ilya Sutskever and Geoffrey Hinton, caused the field of neural networks to move rapidly from being of only fringe interest in the field of Artificial Intelligence, to take centre stage, transforming AI application after AI application – speech recognition, facial recognition, text translation, stock market prediction, and so on.

The possibility of similar "overhang breakthroughs" in AI research – perhaps arising from any of the items in the rich "supply pipeline" I listed in the chapter "The question of urgency" – means that AGI could arise considerably sooner than would be predicted from a cursory look at existing trends of progress.

In other words, the Metaculus predictions may not be so crazy after all!

Alternative canary signals for AGI

The Metaculus questions mentioned above include their own tests for how progress toward AGI can be recognised. Different researchers have made alternative proposals. That is to be welcomed. In each case, a discussion about the new milestones proposed can shed light on risks and opportunities ahead. Again in each case, when progress toward the proposed milestone is either faster than expected or slower than expected, it's a reason for analysts to reflect on their assumptions and, probably, to revise them.

As a good example of a set of milestones that appear both clear and challenging, consider this recent proposal by AI researcher Gary Marcus[164], which lists five possible canary signals:

(1) Whether AI is able to watch a movie and tell you accurately what is going on. Who are the characters? What are their conflicts and motivations? etc.

(2) Whether AI is able to read a novel and reliably answer questions about plot, character, conflicts, motivations, etc.

(3) Whether AI is able to work as a competent cook in an arbitrary kitchen (extending Steve Wozniak's cup of coffee benchmark[165]).

(4) Whether AI is able to reliably construct bug-free code of more than 10,000 lines from natural language specification or by interactions with a non-expert user. (Gluing together code from existing libraries doesn't count.)

(5) Whether AI is able to take arbitrary proofs from the mathematical literature written in natural language and convert them into a symbolic form suitable for symbolic verification.

AI index reports

A different approach to measuring progress with AI is taken by a number of organisations that regularly publish their own reports. These are worth reviewing for signs of change from year to year – and for the reasons given for these changes.

Examples include:

- The AI Index published by Stanford University[166]
- The Global AI Index published by Tortoise Media[167]
- The AI Index Report published by the OECD[168].

A potential shortcoming of these reports is the extent to which they prioritise descriptions of current AI capabilities (and the threats and opportunities arising), rather than forecasts of potential future developments.

However, better foresight generally arises from better hindsight. Accordingly, a sober assessment of how AI capabilities have improved in the recent past is a vital input to deciding the best advice on the management of future AI capabilities.

7.7 Growing a coalition of the willing

The final question arising is "who?"

The Singularity Principles propose that many things should be "questioned", "clarified", "required", "analysed", "anticipated", "rejected", and "promoted".

Who is going to be doing that questioning, clarifying, requiring, analysing, anticipating, rejecting, and promoting?

And who is going to ensure that

- Groups or individuals are held accountable for any knowing or reckless violation of the principles
- Groups or individuals are financially penalised for spreading dangerously misleading information about their products or solutions
- Sufficient resources are made available to address any shortcomings in adhering to the principles
- Projects are actually halted if they continue to violate the Singularity Principles?

Related, who is going to prevent the consolidation of power in centralised entities that could subsequently misuse that power to seriously damage human flourishing? After all, giving more power to a central authority, so they can vigorously promote and police adherence to the Singularity Principles, risks falling foul of Lord Acton's famous warning[169]: "power tends to corrupt; absolute power corrupts absolutely".

My answer to the "who?" question is: *a coalition of the willing*.

7.7 GROWING A COALITION OF THE WILLING

Different people around the world, in numerous different roles, can find their own parts in this grand project:

- Expressing the ideas in this book in new ways that can reach new audiences
- Building bridges to communities that have at least some shared goals and methods
- Finding ways to place these ideas in the forefront of ongoing discussions
- Boosting the "key success factors" of the project:
    - Public understanding
    - Persistent urgency
    - Reliable action against noncompliance
    - Public funding
    - International support
    - A sense of inclusion and collaboration
- Making progress with the various "questions arising" described in previous chapters:
    - Measuring human flourishing
    - Trustable monitoring
    - Uplifting politics
    - Uplifting education
    - To AGI or not AGI?
    - Measuring progress toward AGI
    - Growing a coalition of the willing

I look forward to seeing various parliamentary bodies, at local, national, and transnational levels, endorsing aspects of the Singularity Principles in their own legislation. At the same time, I look forward to the wider democratic community continuing to

- Monitor what politicians do in their names

- Engage with politicians so that the best insights receive priority attention
- Vote out of office politicians who fail to live up to promises to support human flourishing.

I see particular key roles for transnational bodies such as the EU, ASEAN, the CP TPP, the AU, the G7 (and its successor organisations), and aspects of the UN, the OECD, the World Bank, the ISO, and others.

I also anticipate partnerships from organisations representing the sets of professions that I mentioned, in this book's preface, as having contributed numerous ideas that are expressed in the Singularity Principles:

- Scientists, technologists, and engineers
- Entrepreneurs, designers, and artists
- Humanitarians, activists, and lawyers
- Educators, psychologists, and economists
- Philosophers, rationalists, and effective altruists
- Historians, sociologists, and forecasters
- Ethicists, transhumanists, and singularitarians.

Risks and actions

One risk with any extended coalition is that useful activities can become drowned out by a cacophony of noise. It's easy to exchange plenty of words, but it's much harder to inspire and enable practical steps forward.

Addressing this risk requires the discipline of project management. That's a discipline which is sometimes maligned. But, done well, it can make all the difference between good intentions that just produce frustration, and

7.7 Growing a coalition of the willing

good intentions that combine to make a real difference in the world. *World-class project managers, please step forward!*

Alongside world-class project managers, people with outstanding skills in the following disciplines could also make a decisive difference to the overall project:

- Designing, introducing, operating, and evolving regulatory systems that are both agile (adaptive) and lean (carefully targeted)
- Analysing and influencing power structures – the sometimes-hidden forces that often obstruct changes but, on other occasions, accelerate them.

Another risk with any extended coalition is that everyone hangs back, procrastinating, waiting for someone else to take the lead.

To address that risk, I will continue to issue calls to action.

Here's the first such call: if you have read this far, please recommend this book to your friends and colleagues. Write reviews about it online. Arrange events where the ideas of the Singularity Principles can reach wider audiences. And pick one or more items in the set of activities listed above, as something where you can make a difference, *or where you can inspire and assist others*.

To support this extended coalition, I happily offer the services of two organisations whose activities I direct:

- Transpolitica[170] – "*Anticipating tomorrow's politics*"
- London Futurists[171] – "*Serious analysis of radical scenarios for the next 40 years*".

It is said that the best way to predict positive future scenarios is to create that future ourselves. Let's get to it!

Endnotes

Note: For the convenience of readers, the online page https://transpolitica.org/projects/the-singularity-principles/endnotes/ provides an easily clickable version of the following list of endnotes.

---

[1] London Futurists: "Previous meetings" https://londonfuturists.com/previous-meetings/
[2] "History of London Futurists" https://londonfuturists.com/2016/07/10/about-london-futurists/
[3] David W. Wood: *Vital Foresight: The Case For Active Transhumanism* https://transpolitica.org/projects/vital-foresight/
[4] Meetup: "London Futurists" https://www.meetup.com/London-Futurists/
[5] "Books authored or edited by David Wood" https://deltawisdom.com/books/
[6] "Eclectic thoughts on technologies, markets, innovation, openness, collaboration, disruption, risks, and solutions" https://dw2blog.com/
[7] Delta Wisdom: "Radical real-world futurism" https://deltawisdom.com/
[8] Wikipedia: "There's Plenty of Room at the Bottom" https://en.wikipedia.org/wiki/There%27s_Plenty_of_Room_at_the_Bottom
[9] dw2blog: "A wiser journey to a better Tomorrowland" https://dw2blog.com/2015/09/15/a-wiser-journey-to-a-better-tomorrowland/
[10] Dan Milmo, The Guardian: "Rohingya sue Facebook for £150bn over Myanmar genocide" https://www.theguardian.com/technology/2021/dec/06/rohingya-sue-facebook-myanmar-genocide-us-uk-legal-action-social-media-violence

[11] Wikiquote: "Upton Sinclair" https://en.wikiquote.org/wiki/Upton_Sinclair
[12] Science Museum: "Thalidomide" https://www.sciencemuseum.org.uk/objects-and-stories/medicine/thalidomide
[13] React: "The global threat of antibiotic resistance" https://www.reactgroup.org/antibiotic-resistance/the-threat/
[14] Environmental Protection Agency: "DDT – A Brief History and Status" https://www.epa.gov/ingredients-used-pesticide-products/ddt-brief-history-and-status
[15] Tim Harford, BBC News: "Why did we use leaded petrol for so long?" https://www.bbc.co.uk/news/business-40593353
[16] "Asbestos Cover-Up" https://www.asbestos.com/featured-stories/cover-up/
[17] UK Research and Innovation: "The story behind the discovery of the ozone hole" https://www.ukri.org/news-and-events/responding-to-climate-change/topical-stories/the-story-behind-the-discovery-of-the-ozone-hole/
[18] Olivia Smith, New Security Beat: "Big Dams, Big Damage: The Growing Risk of Failure" https://www.newsecuritybeat.org/2018/08/big-dams-big-damage-growing-risk-failure/
[19] World Nuclear Association: "Chernobyl Accident 1986" https://world-nuclear.org/information-library/safety-and-security/safety-of-plants/chernobyl-accident.aspx
[20] Jay Elwes, Prospect: "Financial weapons of mass destruction: Brexit and the looming derivatives threat" https://www.prospectmagazine.co.uk/economics-and-finance/financial-weapons-of-mass-destruction-brexit-and-the-looming-derivatives-threat
[21] The Vital Syllabus: "Transhumanism" https://londonfuturists.com/education/transhumanism/
[22] Anders Sandberg, Aleph: "Definitions of Transhumanism"

https://web.archive.org/web/19970712091927/http://www.aleph.se/Trans/Intro/definitions.html
[23] Michael Eisen: "Amazon's $23,698,655.93 book about flies" https://www.michaeleisen.org/blog/?p=358
[24] AutoML: "What is AutoML?" https://www.automl.org/automl/
[25] AutoML: "Team" https://www.automl.org/team/
[26] Tom Simonite, Wired: "Google's Learning Software Learns to Write Learning Software" https://www.wired.com/story/googles-learning-software-learns-to-write-learning-software/
[27] Will Owen, Venture Beat: "AI tech drives transformation of F1 racing" https://venturebeat.com/2021/11/14/ai-tech-drives-transformation-of-f1-racing/
[28] Pallav Aggarwal: "Automated PCB design using Artificial Intelligence (AI)" https://pallavaggarwal.in/automated-pcb-design-using-ai/
[29] Jonah Comstock, Pharma Phorum: "Insilico's AI-discovered, AI-designed IPF drug enters Phase 1 trials" https://pharmaphorum.com/news/insilicos-ai-discovered-ai-designed-ipf-drug-enters-phase-1-trials/
[30] European Defence Agency: "Stronger communication & radar systems with help of AI" https://eda.europa.eu/news-and-events/news/2020/08/31/stronger-communication-radar-systems-with-help-of-ai
[31] Richard W. Byrne and Nadia Corp, Proceedings of the Royal Society B: Biological Sciences: "Neocortex size predicts deception rate in primates" https://www.ncbi.nlm.nih.gov/pmc/articles/PMC1691785/
[32] Stuart Russell: *Human Compatible: Artificial Intelligence and the Problem of Control* https://www.goodreads.com/book/show/44767248-human-compatible

[33] IMDb: "Dr. Strangelove or: How I Learned to Stop Worrying and Love the Bomb"
https://www.imdb.com/title/tt0057012/
[34] Corporate Finance Institute: "Flash Crashes"
https://corporatefinanceinstitute.com/resources/knowledge/finance/flash-crashes/
[35] Nicole Perlroth: *This Is How They Tell Me the World Ends: The Cyberweapons Arms Race*
https://www.goodreads.com/book/show/49247043-this-is-how-they-tell-me-the-world-ends
[36] Wikipedia: "Tay (bot)"
https://en.wikipedia.org/wiki/Tay_(bot)
[37] Leo Gao, Twitter:
https://twitter.com/nabla_theta/status/1502783399622111234
[38] Rob Bensinger, Twitter:
https://twitter.com/robbensinger/status/1503220020175769602
[39] Wikipedia: "Halting problem"
https://en.wikipedia.org/wiki/Halting_problem
[40] Stephen M. Omohundro: "The Basic AI Drives"
https://selfawaresystems.files.wordpress.com/2008/01/ai_drives_final.pdf
[41] Bruce Schneier: "Snooping on Text by Listening to the Keyboard"
https://www.schneier.com/blog/archives/2005/09/snooping_on_tex.html
[42] Wikipedia: "Three Laws of Robotics"
https://en.wikipedia.org/wiki/Three_Laws_of_Robotics
[43] Wikipedia: "Trolley problem"
https://en.wikipedia.org/wiki/Trolley_problem
[44] Social Progress Imperative: "Index Action Impact"
https://www.socialprogress.org/
[45] Wikipedia: "Goodhart's law"
https://en.wikipedia.org/wiki/Goodhart%27s_law

[46] Wikipedia: "Campbell's law"
https://en.wikipedia.org/wiki/Campbell%27s_law
[47] Science Direct: "Gaia Hypothesis"
https://www.sciencedirect.com/topics/earth-and-planetary-sciences/gaia-hypothesis
[48] Nick Bostrom: "Are You Living In a Computer Simulation?" https://www.simulation-argument.com/
[49] Ray Kurzweil: "The Law of Accelerating Returns" https://www.kurzweilai.net/the-law-of-accelerating-returns
[50] Stanislaw Ulam, American Mathematics Society: "John von Neumann, 1903-1957"
https://www.ams.org/journals/bull/1958-64-03/S0002-9904-1958-10189-5/S0002-9904-1958-10189-5.pdf
[51] Tim Harford, Forbes: "A Beautiful Theory"
https://www.forbes.com/2006/12/10/business-game-theory-tech-cx_th_games06_1212harford.html
[52] William Poundstone: *Prisoner's Dilemma: John von Neumann, Game Theory, and the Puzzle of the Bomb*
https://www.goodreads.com/book/show/29506.Prisoner_s_Dilemma
[53] Wikipedia: "Schrödinger's cat"
https://en.wikipedia.org/wiki/Schr%C3%B6dinger%27s_cat
[54] Greg Hammett: "James Clerk Maxwell, essay on Determinism and Free Will (1873)"
https://w3.pppl.gov/~hammett/Maxwell/freewill.html
[55] Wikipedia: "Maxwell's equations"
https://en.wikipedia.org/wiki/Maxwell%27s_equations
[56] Singularity Group: "Our mission"
https://www.su.org/about
[57] Ray Kurzweil, Penguin Books: "An Excerpt From The Singularity Is Near"
https://web.archive.org/web/20180923051145/https://www.penguin.com/ajax/books/excerpt/9780143037880

Endnotes

[58] Alan Turing: "'Intelligent machinery, a heretical theory', a lecture given to '51 Society' at Manchester" https://turingarchive.kings.cam.ac.uk/publications-lectures-and-talks-amtb/amt-b-4

[59] Wikipedia: "Vernor Vinge" https://en.wikipedia.org/wiki/Vernor_Vinge

[60] Nikola Danaylov, Singularity Weblog: "When Vernor Vinge Coined the Technological Singularity" https://www.singularityweblog.com/when-vernor-vinge-coined-the-technological-singularity/

[61] Vernor Vinge: "The Coming Technological Singularity: How to Survive in the Post-Human Era" https://edoras.sdsu.edu/~vinge/misc/singularity.html

[62] David Brin: "Singularities and Nightmares: Extremes of Optimism and Pessimism About the Human Future" http://www.davidbrin.com/nonfiction/singularity.html

[63] Wikipedia: "David Brin" https://en.wikipedia.org/wiki/David_Brin

[64] LinkedIn: "David Wood: Futurist, catalyst, author, singularitarian" https://www.linkedin.com/in/dw2cco/

[65] OpenAI: "Jukebox" https://openai.com/blog/jukebox/

[66] OpenAI: "DALL·E 2" https://openai.com/dall-e-2/

[67] Carlos E. Perez, Medium: "AlphaZero: How Intuition Demolished Logic" https://medium.com/intuitionmachine/alphazero-how-intuition-demolished-logic-66a4841e6810

[68] Ferris Jabr, Scientific American: "Does Thinking Really Hard Burn More Calories?" https://www.scientificamerican.com/article/thinking-hard-calories/

[69] Intel: "Neuromorphic Computing: Beyond Today's AI" https://www.intel.com/content/www/us/en/research/neuromorphic-computing.html

[70] Hello Future (Orange): "Towards a less data and energy intensive AI"

https://hellofuture.orange.com/en/towards-a-less-data-and-energy-intensive-ai/
[71] Wikipedia: "William Thomson, 1st Baron Kelvin" https://en.wikipedia.org/wiki/William_Thomson,_1st_Baron_Kelvin
[72] Zapatopi: "Interview: Utter Impracticability of Aeronautics & Favorable Opinion on Wireless" http://zapatopi.net/kelvin/papers/interview_aeronautics_and_wireless.html
[73] Tony Czarnecki, Sustensis: "Immature Superintelligence" https://sustensis.co.uk/malevolent-immature-superintelligence/
[74] Wikipedia: "Great Disappointment" https://en.wikipedia.org/wiki/Great_Disappointment
[75] Jo Walton, Tor: "Murder in deep time: Vernor Vinge's *Marooned in Realtime*" https://www.tor.com/2009/08/07/vernor-vinges-marooned-in-realtime/
[76] Graeme MacKay, MacKay Cartoons: "Be sure to wash your hands and all will be well" https://i0.wp.com/mackaycartoons.net/wp-content/uploads/2020/03/2020-0311-NATrevised2sm.jpg
[77] Graeme MacKay, MacKay Cartoons: "Wednesday March 11, 2020" https://mackaycartoons.net/2020/03/18/wednesday-march-11-2020/
[78] Alexander Kruel, Twitter https://twitter.com/XiXiDu/status/1261607019720646657
[79] Wikipedia: "*The Denial of Death*" https://en.wikipedia.org/wiki/The_Denial_of_Death
[80] Vital Syllabus: "Top Level Areas" https://londonfuturists.com/education/vital-syllabus/
[81] Rob Toews, Forbes: "Synthetic Data Is About To Transform Artificial Intelligence"

https://www.forbes.com/sites/robtoews/2022/06/12/synthetic-data-is-about-to-transform-artificial-intelligence/
[82] Hal Hodson, New Scientist: "Google's DeepMind AI can lip-read TV shows better than a pro"
https://www.newscientist.com/article/2113299-googles-deepmind-ai-can-lip-read-tv-shows-better-than-a-pro/
[83] Stanislas Dehaene: *How We Learn: Why Brains Learn Better Than Any Machine... for Now*
https://www.goodreads.com/book/show/46064083-how-we-learn
[84] Cade Metz, The New York Times: "Meet GPT-3. It Has Learned to Code (and Blog and Argue)."
https://www.nytimes.com/2020/11/24/science/artificial-intelligence-ai-gpt3.html
[85] Greg Maxwell, YCombinator Hacker News: "It seems that GPT-3 has its own sense of humor, more of an anti-humor in fact. It is better in bulk."
https://news.ycombinator.com/item?id=24007784
[86] Jason Brownlee, Machine Learning Mastery: "18 Impressive Applications of Generative Adversarial Networks (GANs)"
https://machinelearningmastery.com/impressive-applications-of-generative-adversarial-networks/
[87] Insilico Medicine, "Combining GANs and reinforcement learning for drug discovery"
https://www.eurekalert.org/pub_releases/2018-05/imi-cga050918.php
[88] Wikipedia: "Genetic algorithm"
https://en.wikipedia.org/wiki/Genetic_algorithm
[89] Sam Shead, Business Insider: "The incredible life of DeepMind founder Demis Hassabis, the computer whiz who sold his AI lab to Google for £400 million"
https://www.businessinsider.com/the-incredible-life-of-deepmind-cofounder-demis-hassabis-2017-5
[90] Demis Hassabis, Dharshan Kumaran, Christopher Summerfield, and Matt Botvinick, DeepMind:

"Neuroscience-Inspired Artificial Intelligence" https://www.deepmind.com/publications/neuroscience-inspired-artificial-intelligence

[91] Jeff Hawkins: *A Thousand Brains: A New Theory of Intelligence* https://www.goodreads.com/book/show/54503521-a-thousand-brains

[92] Liqun Luo, Nautilus: "Why Is the Human Brain So Efficient?" http://nautil.us/issue/59/connections/why-is-the-human-brain-so-efficient

[93] Intel: "Neuromorphic Computing: Beyond Today's AI" https://www.intel.co.uk/content/www/uk/en/research/neuromorphic-computing.html

[94] Will Knight, MIT Technology Review: "Quantum computing should supercharge this machine-learning technique" https://www.technologyreview.com/2019/03/13/136628/quantum-computing-should-supercharge-this-machine-learning-technique/

[95] BBVA: "How may quantum computing affect Artificial Intelligence?" https://www.bbva.com/en/how-may-quantum-computing-affect-artificial-intelligence/

[96] Affectiva: "Humanizing technology to bridge the gap between humans and machines" https://www.affectiva.com/

[97] Mark Solms: *The Hidden Spring: A Journey to the Source of Consciousness* https://www.goodreads.com/book/show/53642061-the-hidden-spring

[98] Susan Schneider: *Artificial You: AI and the Future of Your Mind* https://www.goodreads.com/book/show/44526011-artificial-you

[99] Anil Seth: *Being You: A New Science of Consciousness* https://www.goodreads.com/book/show/53036979-being-you

[100] David J. Chalmers: *Reality+: Virtual Worlds and the Problems of Philosophy*
https://www.goodreads.com/book/show/58085215-reality

[101] Judea Pearl and Dana Mackenzie: *The Book of Why: The New Science of Cause and Effect*
https://www.goodreads.com/book/show/36204378-the-book-of-why

[102] Jesus Rodriguez, Medium: "A Gentle Introduction to Probabilistic Programming Languages"
https://medium.com/swlh/a-gentle-introduction-to-probabilistic-programming-languages-bf1e19042ab6

[103] Stuart Russell, CogX2021: "Cutting Edge: The next wave: Probabilistic programming"
https://www.youtube.com/watch?v=YYFbPQiLlxk

[104] "About SingularityNET"
https://singularitynet.io/aboutus/

[105] Steven Levy, Wired: "Mark Zuckerberg on Facebook's Future, From Virtual Reality to Anonymity"
https://www.wired.com/2014/04/zuckerberg-f8-interview/

[106] Stuart Russell: *Human Compatible: Artificial Intelligence and the Problem of Control*
https://www.goodreads.com/book/show/44767248-human-compatible

[107] Kai-Fu Lee and Chen Qiufan, Big Think: "What AI cannot do"
https://bigthink.com/the-future/what-ai-cannot-do/

[108] Adam Satariano and Cade Metz, New York Times: "A Warehouse Robot Learns to Sort Out the Tricky Stuff"
https://www.nytimes.com/2020/01/29/technology/warehouse-robot.html

[109] Wikipedia: "Christopher Columbus"
https://en.wikipedia.org/wiki/Christopher_Columbus

[110] Wikipedia: "Bartolomeu Dias"
https://en.wikipedia.org/wiki/Bartolomeu_Dias

[111] Irving John Good: "Speculations Concerning the First Ultraintelligent Machine" http://web.archive.org/web/20010527181244/http://www.aeiveos.com/~bradbury/Authors/Computing/Good-IJ/SCtFUM.html

[112] I. J. Good, "Speculations on Perceptrons and other Automata" https://dominoweb.draco.res.ibm.com/reports/rc115.pdf

[113] Wikipedia: "68–95–99.7 rule" https://en.wikipedia.org/wiki/68%E2%80%9395%E2%80%9399.7_rule

[114] Peter Thal Larsen, Financial Times: "Goldman pays the price of being big" https://www.ft.com/content/d2121cb6-49cb-11dc-9ffe-0000779fd2ac

[115] John B. Taylor and John C. Williams, Federal Reserve Bank of San Francisco: "A Black Swan in the Money Market" https://www.frbsf.org/economic-research/files/wp08-04bk.pdf

[116] Dawn Connelly, The Pharmaceutical Journal: "A history of aspirin" https://pharmaceutical-journal.com/article/infographics/a-history-of-aspirin

[117] Wikipedia: "Category: Drugs with unknown mechanisms of action" https://en.wikipedia.org/wiki/Category:Drugs_with_unknown_mechanisms_of_action

[118] Matt Turek, Darpa: "Explainable Artificial Intelligence (XAI)" https://www.darpa.mil/program/explainable-artificial-intelligence

[119] Arvind Narayanan: "Tutorial: 21 fairness definitions and their policies" https://www.youtube.com/watch?v=jIXIuYdnyyk

[120] Javier Zarracina, Vox: "The case against equality of opportunity" https://www.vox.com/2015/9/21/9334215/equality-of-opportunity

ENDNOTES

[121] Peter Strozniak, Industry Week: "Toyota Alters Face Of Production"
https://www.industryweek.com/operations/continuous-improvement/article/21947002/toyota-alters-face-of-production

[122] JBS Haldane: "Daedalus, or, Science and the Future"
https://www.marxists.org/archive/haldane/works/1920s/daedalus.htm

[123] David W. Wood: *Sustainable Superabundance: A Universal Transhumanist Invitation*
https://transpolitica.org/projects/abundance-manifesto/

[124] Daniel Susskind: *A World Without Work: Technology, Automation, and How We Should Respond*
https://www.goodreads.com/book/show/51300408-a-world-without-work

[125] The United Nations: "Universal Declaration of Human Rights" https://www.un.org/en/about-us/universal-declaration-of-human-rights

[126] Wikipedia: "Universal Declaration of Human Rights"
https://en.wikipedia.org/wiki/Universal_Declaration_of_Human_Rights

[127] David W. Wood: *Sustainable Superabundance: A Universal Transhumanist Invitation*
https://transpolitica.org/projects/abundance-manifesto/

[128] David W. Wood: "Introduction to Landmines"
https://www.youtube.com/watch?v=6zsUedvrVnY

[129] UK Office for National Statistics: "Well-being"
https://www.ons.gov.uk/peoplepopulationandcommunity/wellbeing/

[130] pjammer: "Accelerating Change 2005"
https://web.archive.org/web/20060327005000/http://pjammer.livejournal.com/151502.html

[131] Nick Bostrom: "The Vulnerable World Hypothesis"
https://nickbostrom.com/papers/vulnerable.pdf

[132] Mothers Against Drunk Driving: "No More Victims"
https://www.madd.org/

[133] Investigatory Powers Commissioner's Office
https://www.ipco.org.uk/
[134] The Intelligence and Security Committee of Parliament
https://isc.independent.gov.uk/
[135] Bruce Schneier, New York Intelligencer: "Click Here to Kill Everyone"
https://nymag.com/intelligencer/2017/01/the-internet-of-things-dangerous-future-bruce-schneier.html
[136] David W. Wood: "Transcending Politics Preview"
https://www.youtube.com/watch?v=5lJYyEdiwOM
[137] Thomas W. Malone: *Superminds: The Surprising Power of People and Computers Thinking Together*
https://www.goodreads.com/book/show/36204268-superminds
[138] David W. Wood: *Transcending Politics: A Technoprogressive Roadmap to a Comprehensively Better Future*
https://transpolitica.org/projects/transcending-politics/
[139] Vital Syllabus: "Top Level Areas"
https://londonfuturists.com/education/vital-syllabus/
[140] Vital Syllabus: "FAQ"
https://londonfuturists.com/education/vital-syllabus/faq/
[141] Clemency Burton-Hill, The Guardian: "The superhero of artificial intelligence: can this genius keep it in check?"
https://www.theguardian.com/technology/2016/feb/16/demis-hassabis-artificial-intelligence-deepmind-alphago
[142] David Silver, Satinder Singh, Doina Precup, and Richard S. Sutton, Artificial Intelligence: "Reward is enough"
https://www.sciencedirect.com/science/article/pii/S0004370221000862
[143] Scott Alexander, Astral Codex Ten: "My Bet: AI Size Solves Flubs" https://astralcodexten.substack.com/p/my-bet-ai-size-solves-flubs
[144] Herbert A. Simon and Allen Newell, Operations Research: "Heuristic Problem Solving: The Next Advance

in Operations Research"
https://pubsonline.informs.org/doi/abs/10.1287/opre.6.1.1
[145] A.M. Turing Award: "Allen Newell, United States – 1975"
https://amturing.acm.org/award_winners/newell_3167755.cfm
[146] The Nobel Prize: "Press release: Studies of Decision-Making lead to Prize in Economics"
https://www.nobelprize.org/prizes/economic-sciences/1978/press-release/
[147] Alan Levinovitz, Wired: "The Mystery of Go, the Ancient Game That Computers Still Can't Win"
https://www.wired.com/2014/05/the-world-of-computer-go/
[148] Cade Metz, Wired: "What the AI behind AlphaGo can teach us about being human"
https://www.wired.com/2016/05/google-alpha-go-ai/
[149] Metaculus: "Welcome!" https://www.metaculus.com/
[150] Anthony Aguirre, Future of Life Institute: "Predicting the Future (of Life)"
https://futureoflife.org/2016/01/24/predicting-the-future-of-life/
[151] IARPA: "ACE: Aggregative Contingent Estimation"
http://www.iarpa.gov/index.php/research-programs/ace
[152] Good Judgment: "See the future sooner"
https://goodjudgment.com/
[153] Metaculus: "FAQ"
https://www.metaculus.com/help/faq/
[154] Metaculus: "Date Weakly General AI is Publicly Known"
https://www.metaculus.com/questions/3479/date-weakly-general-ai-system-is-devised/
[155] Metaculus: "'Silver' Turing Test be passed by 2026"
https://www.metaculus.com/questions/73/will-the-silver-turing-test-be-passed-by-2026/

[156] Metaculus: "What will be the best score in the 2019/2020 Winograd Schema AI challenge" https://www.metaculus.com/questions/644/what-will-be-the-best-score-in-the-20192020-winograd-schema-ai-challenge/

[157] Keisuke Sakaguchi, Ronan Le Bras, Chandra Bhagavatula, and Yejin Choi, Computer Science: "WinoGrande: An Adversarial Winograd Schema Challenge at Scale" https://arxiv.org/abs/1907.10641

[158] Metaculus: "Date of Artificial General Intelligence" https://www.metaculus.com/questions/5121/date-of-general-ai/

[159] Model Space: "Ferrari 312 T4 | 1:8 Model | Full Kit" https://web.archive.org/web/20210613075708/https://www.model-space.com/us/build-the-ferrari-312-t4-model-car.html

[160] Dan Hendrycks, Collin Burns, Steven Basart, Andy Zou, Mantas Mazeika, Dawn Song, and Jacob Steinhardt, Computer Science: "Measuring Massive Multitask Language Understanding" https://arxiv.org/abs/2009.03300

[161] Dan Hendrycks, Steven Basart, Saurav Kadavath, Mantas Mazeika, Akul Arora, Ethan Guo, Collin Burns, Samir Puranik, Horace He, Dawn Song, and Jacob Steinhardt, Computer Science: "Measuring Coding Challenge Competence With APPS" https://arxiv.org/abs/2105.09938

[162] J. Mehra: "'Golden Age of Theoretical Physics': P.A.M Dirac's Scientific Work from 1924 to 1933" https://www.osti.gov/servlets/purl/4661346

[163] Theodosius Dobzhansky, The American Biology Teacher: "Nothing in Biology Makes Sense Except in the Light of Evolution" https://www.pbs.org/wgbh/evolution/library/10/2/text_pop/l_102_01.html

[164] Gary Marcus, Substack: "Dear Elon Musk, here are five things you might want to consider about AGI" https://garymarcus.substack.com/p/dear-elon-musk-here-are-five-things

[165] Michael Shick, Fast Company: "Wozniak: Could a Computer Make a Cup of Coffee?" https://www.fastcompany.com/1568187/wozniak-could-computer-make-cup-coffee

[166] Stanford University AI Index: "Ground the conversation about AI in data" https://aiindex.stanford.edu/

[167] Tortoise Media: "The Global AI Index" https://www.tortoisemedia.com/intelligence/global-ai/

[168] OECD AI Policy Observatory: "AI Index Report 2021" https://oecd.ai/en/wonk/documents/ai-index-report-2021

[169] Lord Acton Quote Archive: "Power and Authority" https://www.acton.org/research/lord-acton-quote-archive

[170] Transpolitica: "Anticipating tomorrow's politics" https://transpolitica.org/

[171] London Futurists: "Serious analysis of radical scenarios for the next 40 years" https://londonfuturists.com/